Introduction

On 18 February 1943 Nazi Propaganda Minister Joseph Goebbels made a speech in the Berlin Sports Palace that is generally regarded as one of the most chilling, and at the same time most effective, rhetorical performances of the twentieth century. It is held to exemplify the particularly insidious nature of National Socialist propaganda. A comment from 2013 in the newspaper *Die Welt* is typical: the speech is a 'rhetorical masterpiece', a successful 'coup', while 'total war', it is claimed, prolonged the life of the Third Reich by many months. Rafael Seligmann called this shoddy piece of propaganda 'probably the most impressive display of the power of political suggestion in world history', which sent a 'psychological shockwave through Germany...with significant material and political consequences'.[1] Documentaries about the 'Third Reich' repeatedly use the historic newsreel footage with the famous/infamous question about 'total war' and the ensuing deafening endorsement offered by a seemingly mesmerized audience. A good number of school textbooks print verbatim the ten questions in which the speech culminated and ask pupils to analyse the content and rhetorical techniques of the passage.[2]

Three factors above all account for the Sports Palace event remaining so alive in the collective memory, even after eighty years.

First of all, it is regarded as the classic example of National Socialist propaganda—a mass rally perfectly staged at a highly symbolic venue and broadcast throughout the world by means of press, radio, and newsreel using the most elaborate communications systems available.

Second: the speech is frequently cited as a perfidious masterpiece produced by the Nazis' propagandist-in-chief Joseph Goebbels and a particularly extreme example of his modus operandi. It demonstrates, it is claimed, how this highly intelligent, ice-cold, and boundlessly fanatical demagogue pressed all the right buttons with positively diabolical skill.

The speech thus seems the ultimate expression of the almost legendary 'Goebbels propaganda', still a synonym for a brazen and incendiary tissue of lies. To this day, and not only in Germany, to be said to distort the truth 'like Goebbels' is a weighty accusation, the ultimate weapon, as it were, in the arsenal of political polemic.

Third: the speech is widely regarded as a prime example of 'mass suggestion', of the almost limitless capacity of a deluded audience, utterly at the mercy of a barrage of propaganda, to be manipulated and seduced. A roaring crowd demands 'total war', wants it to be 'more total', and willingly follows the speaker, who declares 'the most total' to be 'just about total enough' for 'now'. Whipped up into fanaticism, the crowd appears ready to plunge over the cliff like the proverbial lemmings. For this reason, the rally of 18 February 1943 exerts to this day a peculiar fascination, seeming as it does to confirm in particular the claim that the German population of the time was almost zombie-like in the face of the propaganda machine. This 'seduction theory' then offers a supposedly plausible explanation for the Germans' continued support for the regime in spite of all its crimes and atrocities. Thus the rally seems to provide outstanding historical evidence to support the view that in the modern world if you control the media totally you can control the minds of the vast majority to suit your own ends.

In employing the expression 'total war', so central to the Sports Palace rally, Goebbels was using a term that in the second half of the 1930s in Germany was regarded as the key to success in any future war. This term spread above all as a result of a publication with the same title by Erich Ludendorff, the former World War I quartermaster general. Appearing in 1935, in its day it aroused considerable interest, giving rise to numerous further publications and making the term a popular slogan.[3] In particular, Ludendorff linked two conceptions. On the one hand, numerous authors in the 1920s had analysed the experiences of World War I and concluded that the 'war of the future' could be waged successfully only by subordinating all areas of life systematically to its demands. That meant in particular moving production as a whole onto an efficient war economy footing, exercising complete control over the deployment of the workforce, conducting a propaganda war internally as well as externally, and creating an absolutely united 'home front'. Ideally, these aims should already have been

GOEBBELS AND 'TOTAL WAR'

THE SPORTS PALACE SPEECH OF 1943

PETER LONGERICH

Translated by

LESLEY SHARPE

AND

JEREMY NOAKES

OXFORD
UNIVERSITY PRESS

OXFORD
UNIVERSITY PRESS

Great Clarendon Street, Oxford, OX2 6DP,
United Kingdom

Oxford University Press is a department of the University of Oxford.
It furthers the University's objective of excellence in research, scholarship,
and education by publishing worldwide. Oxford is a registered trade mark of
Oxford University Press in the UK and in certain other countries.

Translation by Lesley Sharpe and Jeremy Noakes, 2025

The moral rights of the authors have been asserted.

Published in the United States of America by Oxford University Press
198 Madison Avenue, New York, NY 10016, United States of America

British Library Cataloguing in Publication Data

Data available

Library of Congress Control Number: 2025935495

ISBN 9780198923770

DOI: 10.1093/oso/9780198923770.001.0001

Printed and bound by
CPI Group (UK) Ltd., Croydon, CR0 4YY

MIX
Paper | Supporting
responsible forestry
FSC
www.fsc.org
FSC® C013604

The manufacturer's authorised representative in the EU for product safety is
Oxford University Press España S.A. of Parque Empresarial San Fernando de Henares,
Avenida de Castilla, 2 − 28830 Madrid (www.oup.es/en or product.safety@oup.com).
OUP España S.A. also acts as importer into Spain of products made by the manufacturer.

Contents

Introduction   1

1. Before the speech: From hopes of victory in summer
   1942 to the winter crisis of 1942/3   4
2. Goebbels's speech on 'total war': Text and commentary   40
3. After the speech   97

Acknowledgements   123
List of archives used   125
Notes   127
Bibliography   141
Index   145

achieved in peacetime by radically transforming state and society to create a 'defence community', backed up by intensive training and education.[4]

Adopting these ideas, Ludendorff claimed that the 'issue of how to supply the nation and the armed forces' could certainly 'be solved . . . by technical and organizational measures'.[5] However, the chief problem posed by total war was how to create 'a unity of hearts and minds' within the nation (naturally on the basis of their common 'genetic inheritance as a race') and establish strong internal political leadership by a 'supreme commander', who even in peacetime should place politics in the service of war.[6] Thus the slogan 'total war' as Ludendorff conceived of it acquired a decidedly irrational dimension that located it in the tradition of *völkisch* (ethno-nationalist) thought. It combined two components: an immense concentration of effort drawn from the depths of the nation and a national resurgence powered by complete confidence in the extraordinary abilities of a leader chosen by destiny.

The essential elements of this highly charged term are evident in Goebbels's speech: in addition to the concrete organizational measures to subordinate the economy and society in future completely to the war, we find in particular a call for unity within the nation and the appeal for absolute loyalty to the 'Führer'. These elements are combined, as in Ludendorff, with hate-filled polemic against the alleged enemies of unity between the nation and its leadership, namely the Jews. Thus in his speech Goebbels was not making use of a clearly defined idea but rather of a familiar but at the same time elusive and multi-layered concept that comprised an organizational and technical dimension as well as an ethno-nationalist and irrational one.

All these factors combined—the rally, its originator, the extraordinary effect attributed to it, as well as the key term 'total war' used there—certainly provide fertile ground for myth-making. By contrast, historical research[7] has for some time been demythologizing the background and circumstances of this event and situating it in the context of an internal power struggle within the National Socialist system, a system that in February 1943 was facing its greatest crisis. The main focus of this book will therefore also be the political prehistory and the after-effects of the rally. Both will be closely examined in separate chapters. Between these two chapters a further chapter contains the actual text of the speech and a detailed commentary on it.

I

Before the speech

From hopes of victory in summer 1942
to the winter crisis of 1942/3

Goebbels's rally at the Sports Palace on 18 February 1943 was the climax of a campaign for 'total war' that was quite specifically initiated and orchestrated by him as Propaganda Minister. It is inextricably bound up with him as an individual and important character traits and idiosyncrasies of his are reflected in it.[1]

In 1943 Goebbels had been engaged for almost two decades primarily as a propagandist. He had been working since 1924 for the (still banned) Nazi party (NSDAP) as a journalist and speaker. As Gauleiter of Berlin from 1926 onwards he had been subjecting the Reich capital to a sustained campaign of strident agitation and unrestrained violence. In addition, in 1931 he became the NSDAP's Reich propaganda chief, organizing his party's subsequent election campaigns. In April 1933 he finally became Reich Minister for National Enlightenment and Propaganda.

Probably the most important personality trait that Goebbels brought to his work as a professional propagandist was one that had its roots in his fundamental narcissism, namely his boundless need for public recognition, an insatiable craving for people to admire his genius. His diaries show that he experienced his ceaseless propaganda activities as an extraordinary sequence of personal successes and emotional high points. This is particularly true of his speaking engagements: descriptions of his numerous rallies at the Sports Palace, for example, almost always contain the comment that the arena with its 10,000 seats was 'packed full', 'packed full as always', or 'yet again even more packed full than ever'[2]—a characteristic formulation he used to raise isolated events to the level of a permanent state of affairs. He almost invariably perceived the audience's reaction as wholly enthusiastic and recorded it with elation in his diary: once again 'thunderous applause', 'waves of wild applause', the audience 'went mad', there was a 'feverish atmosphere', an 'explosive mood', or quite simply 'the purest Sports Palace atmosphere'.[3] When he had made a speech, he always recorded himself as having been 'on top form', 'on splendid form', 'on great form', and the like. After a speech, he enjoyed being entertained with a few other guests and basking in the glow of his recent triumph, and in his diary a day or two after a speaking engagement we regularly find entries showing positively childlike pleasure at the massive positive response evident in the media, even though his own ministry had organized that response and orchestrated it down to the last detail.

His rampant narcissism and elation at his own success were therefore not only an important impulse for Goebbels's restless activity as a propagandist, they also led him hugely to overestimate the quality and impact of his efforts. Goebbels was almost incapable of separating his self-perception from other people's estimation of him. The two coalesced and his desire to have been wonderful yet again was so powerful that in his euphoria he projected his ecstatic experience of his own success onto others' judgement of his performance. The result was megalomania.

As is the case with many narcissists, Goebbels's craving for recognition was linked to his dependence on an attachment figure close to him, who through constant praise and admiration gave him a sense of personal stability. As early as 1924/5, after desperate searching, Goebbels had found this figure in Hitler, who quickly recognized Goebbels's personal weakness and consistently exploited it, keeping up the steady stream of appreciation and encouragement that was existentially necessary to him. If the 'Führer' withheld his favour even briefly, Goebbels was immediately plunged into self-doubt and depression.

In this relationship of deep dependence on Hitler, propaganda for the 'Führer' and the cult of the 'Führer' were not only propaganda strategies but inflated his personal adoration of his idol to mammoth proportions. The idea that he was the man chosen to unite the whole of the German nation behind Adolf Hitler, the man chosen by destiny to save the fatherland, was the real spur to his ceaseless activity.

Goebbels's craving for public recognition and his dependence on Hitler underlie another important factor: his political ambition to extend his role as Hitler's chief propagandist and to become the latter's closest confidant and political ally and the real executor of the Führer's wishes.

Though he was the Gauleiter of Berlin during the 'time of struggle' (the National Socialists' self-aggrandizing term for their rise during the Weimar Republic), Goebbels must have realized that he was not part of the small group of leading figures who accompanied Hitler to the exploratory talks in Berlin that preceded the 'seizure of power' and were privy to his most secret plans. He was not included in the negotiations leading to the Hitler–Papen government in January 1933. Similarly, after the 'seizure of power' he was only sketchily informed about Hitler's decisions on important political matters. Thus in June 1934, when Hitler eliminated the SA leadership around Röhm, he kept Goebbels in the dark about his true intentions up to the very last minute. The latter believed that 'reactionary elements' would be the target. Again, during these years Hitler did not as a rule disclose to Goebbels the details of his thinking on foreign policy, but rather mostly only informed him about his next steps if the propaganda situation required it.

In 1938/9 Goebbels was forced to accept serious damage to his relationship with Hitler and loss of status within the National Socialist power structure. One reason for this was his affair with the actress Lída Baarová. This affair had become public knowledge and Hitler insisted that Goebbels end it and continue with his marriage, even though it had broken down. Even more important for the crisis in the Hitler–Goebbels relationship was the Propaganda Minister's reluctance at the height of the Sudeten crisis in the autumn of 1938 to prime the German population for the war Hitler was pushing for. However, the November pogrom (*Kristallnacht*), in which Hitler had assigned Goebbels the key role, was an important factor in making the latter then fall in with the aggressive course Hitler was taking and change the focus of propaganda completely to preparation for war. Even so, he found that in the competition for the 'Führer's' favour other leading figures in the regime such as Joachim von Ribbentrop or Heinrich Himmler were overtaking him and he continued to play only a marginal role in the real decision-making processes. This was particularly true of Hitler's foreign policy manoeuvres in 1940 and of preparations for the various military 'campaigns'. Thus Goebbels was not aware of the coming invasion of the Soviet Union until March 1941, even though Hitler had been planning it since the summer of 1940 and troop deployments had already begun.

As long as the wars waged by the Third Reich were successful and the news was only of victories, Goebbels was not faced with serious challenges as Propaganda Minister. His moment did not arrive until autumn 1941, when the advance into Russia ground to a halt and the regime found itself in a serious crisis. Now he regarded it as his central task to bolster faltering morale and prime the population for a long war and the resulting privations. He had to call for greater 'toughness' and 'backbone'.[4] He was particularly concerned to suppress any discussion of how long the war was likely to last. As he impressed on the German population, the crucial question was not how long the war would last but how it would end.[5] At the height of the winter crisis, when the troops in the east, lacking kit for winter, finally ground to a halt, he went to great lengths to give the population a keen sense of the seriousness of the situation by organizing a collection of woollen items. Collecting socks and pullovers would at the same time provide people with an occupation to counteract the mood of depression: 'The more the home front has to do, the better will be its morale.' The population, he claimed, was 'happy to make sacrifices and to be involved directly in the war effort'.[6]

The situation in summer 1942

The military situation did in fact become less tense in the course of spring 1942. Indeed, the taking of Tobruk in June along with the German–Italian advance towards the Libyan–Egyptian border and the start of the summer offensive in the east at the end of that month were more hopeful developments. They came, however, at the expense of anti-aircraft capacity in the west, which the RAF exploited to carry out massive raids on German cities. In March Lübeck was heavily bombed, then Rostock in April and Cologne in May, followed by Essen and Bremen in June, Duisburg in July, and Düsseldorf at the beginning of August.[7] Goebbels feared that further bombing raids, military defeats on land, or food shortages over the summer might result in a sudden collapse in the public mood, which in the meantime had been relatively relaxed, bordering on positive. In July and August, therefore, both in his diaries and his propaganda instructions he rejected any exaggerated optimism.[8]

Yet this circumspect approach brought him into conflict with Hitler, who saw the final decisive point in the war as being within sight. On 19 August Goebbels visited the Führer headquarters in Vinnitsa, where in a mood of great optimism Hitler expounded to him his plans for the future: In two to three days, he said, he intended to launch the main attack on Stalingrad; the city on the Volga 'was particularly in his sights', as Goebbels recorded, and his aim was 'to raze it to the ground' for 'psychological reasons as well as for military ones'. He calculated that the city could be taken in a week.[9]

Then, by the autumn at the latest, he intended to use the southern flank of the offensive to take the oil fields of Baku. But that was not all: Hitler was pursuing what Goebbels referred to as the 'gargantuan plan' of 'pushing on into the Near East, conquering Asia Minor, taking Iraq, Iran, and Palestine by surprise, and thus cutting England off from its last oil reserves following the loss of its East Asian sources'. If one added the territories wrested from the 'bolshevists' and vital for their supplies, then 'we will have our hands round the enemy's throat'.

In North Africa Rommel's troops would 'sooner or later break out of their position at El Alamein and advance to Cairo', even though Rommel's first attempt to break out in July had been unsuccessful. As Goebbels, not without a touch of scepticism, commented in a long diary entry about the meeting, the 'gargantuan plan' to take the entire Near East in a pincer movement from the west and the north had 'for the moment to be seen as a distant dream'. Yet at the same time he was evidently impressed with Hitler's determination, seeing it as at least possible that 'the enemy would collapse under the weight of these blows'.

In view of this appraisal of the situation, Hitler told Goebbels he was not in favour of launching 'much in the way of propaganda against the growing optimism', for it would 'even itself out of its own accord'. Hitler had thus addressed the precise issue that had been troubling Goebbels for some weeks. As he had done repeatedly within a short period of time,[10] the day before this meeting he had written a lengthy diary entry criticizing the 'positively grotesque daily increase in excessive optimism in the German population about the situation at the front'. Also, as on the preceding day,[11] he had issued an instruction to that effect to press and radio: 'A failure on our part to convey in timely fashion to the nation the seriousness of the war and its probable duration would result in a severe psychological shock at the end of the autumn.'[12]

There were therefore considerable differences between the dictator and his Propaganda Minister over this matter and these were to become very apparent in the weeks that followed. For the time being, however, the topic was shelved. On the evening of 19 August they conversed about cultural and personal matters as well as various other topics, as had become a kind of ritual during Goebbels's visits to the Führer's headquarters, until Goebbels retired for the night: 'This enjoyable day is now over. I feel refreshed as one does after a bath.'

As Hitler had announced, a few days later, on 23 August, the real battle for Stalingrad began. Amid increasingly stubborn resistance from the Red Army the German troops fought their way to the city's outskirts.[13]

By the middle of September Goebbels had come to the conclusion that 'the fate of this year's summer and autumn campaign' was largely dependent 'on the capture of Stalingrad'.[14] Planning ahead, he issued detailed instructions at his daily ministerial briefing on 15 September for the radio announcement that the city had been taken.

Otto Dietrich, the 'Reich Press Chief', went a step further, however. He was vying keenly with Goebbels over who should give the media their daily instructions and the same day he issued a 'watchword of the day', in which he primed the German press to 'honour in the most striking way possible' the imminent 'victorious outcome of this great struggle for the city of Stalingrad'. Goebbels, though, resisted a comparable wish on Hitler's part to go ahead with a special announcement. Thus the press was informed the following day that 'a number of suboperations' were still in progress and would have to be 'concluded' before the 'fall of Stalingrad'.[15]

This affair revived memories for Goebbels of the previous autumn, when Dietrich, clearly influenced by the overoptimistic atmosphere in the Führer headquarters, made a premature announcement in the media about imminent military victory over the Soviet Union. At first this produced euphoria in the population, followed by deep disappointment when the swift victory failed to happen. Goebbels had attempted at the time to use propaganda to repair the damage Dietrich had done and since then had been at pains to avoid such dangerous fluctuations of mood.[16]

At the ministerial briefing at the end of September 1942 he referred
to Dietrich's news policy as 'incomprehensible and foolish'.[17] The
Reich Press Chief himself was given a dressing down. According to
Goebbels, Dietrich was sheepish, probably because he was conscious of
'the weakness of his position and the wrongheadedness of his news
policy, which has once again led to such embarrassing difficulties and
complications'.[18]

'Excessive optimism' in autumn 1942

Opening the Winter Aid scheme in Berlin on 30 September, Hitler
spoke about the future development of the war; it was his first public
appearance in over five months and was broadcast on the radio. In his
speech he announced the fall of Stalingrad. Assuming final victory
over the Soviet Union he expatiated on the future 'organization of this
gigantic expanse of territory'; he did not say anything about how long
the war might last.[19]

At a meeting the following day of Gauleiters and Reichsleiters
Hitler was again confident of victory. As Goebbels noted, 'for him and
for us there is only total victory or total annihilation, though he wanted
there to be no doubt that total victory was as good as assured'. Hitler
went on to say that his original 'operational and strategic plan' would,
'for the most part', be 'successfully executed militarily' that year. This
plan, he said, had failed the previous year through the incompetence of
the then Commander in Chief of the Army, von Brauchitsch, who had
been dismissed in December 1941. His plan, he continued, 'amounted
to destroying the Soviets' economic foundations and thus eliminating
and crushing them once and for all'. Thereafter he intended to advance
along the Caspian Sea 'to Mesopotamia to leave his calling card at the
English oil bases'.[20]

In October Goebbels continued to be concerned about the 'excessive optimism, not to say illusions' that had re-emerged following
speeches by Göring and other leading politicians.[21] Goebbels tried to
counteract these by instructing propaganda staff 'to present the situation with sober realism so that the German nation is not cast down
sooner or later from seventh heaven onto the hard earth'.[22] In contrast
to Hitler's wide-ranging plans, Goebbels now began to focus the
population on the very practical aspects of the war.

On 12 October he recorded in his diary 'that we must soon begin to put together a programme for the autumn and winter months'. Rather than going on the offensive again, troops on the eastern front would very soon be forced to retreat to a fixed line. This second winter for the war in the east would present the propaganda machine with particular challenges. The response to this situation, he wrote, must be for propaganda

to navigate more and more towards a total and radical kind of war, at home as well as in the field. I hope that there will be a more receptive mood for this approach during the autumn and winter than there was in the summer. I'll then take centre stage again. In the course of the next few months I shall probably succeed in pushing through a whole series of measures that up to now I couldn't push through. ... Although we may speak of total war we aren't as yet waging one in practice. But though we aren't yet, we soon will and must be.

In mid-October and early November Goebbels used his regular column in the weekly *Das Reich* to publish two articles in which he took up what he himself considered to be a 'realistic'[23] position within war propaganda. Under the heading 'The Earth's Blessing' he took an expressly pragmatic line regarding the war aims in the east: 'This time it is not about throne and altar but about grain and oil, about space for our growing population, which cannot live or be fed in the cramped territory it has occupied so far.' Two weeks later, under the heading 'The War as Social Revolution' he asserted: 'In this war we are essentially fighting to gain the preconditions for the completion of our nation's social revolution', whereas the war forced on Germany by 'plutocracy' was a 'challenge to our revolution and in particular to its socialist aspect'.[24]

A crisis is brewing

In the meantime, the prospects of achieving decisive victories over the Soviet Union by the end of the year were fading. All eyes were on the city that bore the Soviet dictator's name. Although by the end of October the German armed forces had occupied almost the whole city, by now completely flattened, they were unable to take the narrow strip of land to the west of the Volga still held by the Red Army; the 6th Army deployed at Stalingrad had no more strength to attack.[25]

In his diaries during the last third of the month Goebbels seemed on the one hand worried about the increasingly critical situation in Stalingrad; on the other, however, he also recorded with a certain satisfaction that the nation had 'finally discarded any illusions about the campaign in the east'. He considered it noteworthy that in place of the slogan 'We shall win!' people were more inclined to say, 'We must win!': 'In general people are conscious that this war is our last chance and we mustn't lose it.'[26]

The situation then became more ominous following the precarious developments in the North African theatre of war. At the beginning of September Rommel had not managed to break through the enemy's lines at Alam Halfa. Then in late October/early November he finally suffered a serious defeat at the second battle of El-Alamein and was forced to retreat rapidly westwards.[27]

Goebbels responded with a further article for the weekly *Das Reich*, in which he made a comparison with the situation immediately before the 'seizure of power'—a subject he would come back to repeatedly in the months that followed and was to crop up again in the Sports Palace speech of 18 February. At the end of 1932, he said, National Socialism had been forced to go it alone and, as today, to fight against an 'odd bunch of cronies', an unnatural coalition of bourgeois and communists. As they had done then, they would in the end win through today too.[28]

He also recommended to the enemy to talk 'less about our mood and more about our bearing'. 'Mood is on the whole the matter of a moment, whereas bearing is something that lasts.' Goebbels used this distinction to begin an important change in how the NS regime steered 'public opinion'. His aim was to make National Socialist policy independent of fluctuations in mood, such as were recorded by the Security Service (SD) of the SS or his own propaganda offices in their regular reports.

Up to then the population's 'mood' had always been an important criterion in judging the success of National Socialist policy—and it was Goebbels who had been chiefly responsible for maintaining it. A 'positive mood' meant that the overwhelming majority of the population was indicating its approval of the regime's policies by its behaviour in public, in other words by regularly attending National Socialist meetings, donating regularly to appeals, using the Hitler greeting, hanging swastika flags from windows, joining in marches or lining the streets to cheer, listening enthusiastically in public spaces to loudspeaker broadcasts of propaganda rallies, and so on. The propaganda media then did their best to reproduce this impression of the nation's complete unity. As the regime enjoyed a media monopoly and, by taking advantage of the extensive Party apparatus, had created a dense system of control, the population's public behaviour could be manipulated to a high degree.

A 'positive mood' could therefore to a great extent be generated, if necessary by harassing 'whingers' and awkward customers or employing more severe measures against them. All of this was very elaborate, however, and not sustainable from day to day in wartime. In particular, as the war went on, big events were largely discontinued, whereas previously every few weeks Reich Party Conferences, May Day celebrations, harvest thanksgivings, ceremonies of dedication, military parades, ceremonial entries, or large-scale march-pasts had provided an opportunity to record the population's unbounded loyalty and immense enthusiasm. Consequently, negative reactions to the regime's policies could less easily be drowned out by the noise of propaganda, while, as we have already seen with Goebbels, an overoptimistic mood in wartime seemed positively irresponsible and could raise unwelcome expectations. For Goebbels it was enough if the population was mindful of the seriousness of the war and fulfilled their everyday duties without becoming apathetic or recalcitrant.

On 8 November, the day on which the article by Goebbels just mentioned appeared, the Party leadership was gathering in Munich, as they did every year, to mark the anniversary of the failed putsch of 1923, when a further piece of bad news arrived: British and American forces had landed in Morocco and Algeria. It soon became clear that the French troops stationed there, who were Vichy French forces, were putting up at best token resistance, giving rise to the fear that Rommel's forces would now be trapped in a pincer movement from both sides.[29] Although Hitler's speech, broadcast on the radio that evening from the Löwenbräukeller in Munich, showed him confident of victory, he mentioned the alarming news from North Africa, though only in passing.[30] The notes in Goebbels's diaries about the activities of the NS leaders on 8 November and the following days give the impression of a certain bewilderment in the face of this new situation.

In order to resist the Allied troops advancing from the west, the German forces rushed to construct a bridgehead in Tunisia, while

Rommel's troops also withdrew towards Tunisia. From 11 November onwards German troops marched into the hitherto unoccupied zone in southern France. Preparations were thus already being made to meet an attempted Allied landing on the Mediterranean coast.[31]

A few days after these events further dramatic news arrived from the eastern front. A Soviet offensive launched on 19 November from the north and east against the arc of the German front at Stalingrad led after only four days to the German 6th Army being encircled. This was at first concealed from the German population. Goebbels knew what it meant: 'This of course puts us in an extraordinarily precarious position. If we don't succeed in breaking through this encirclement our Stalingrad front and the whole of the front on the Volga is under threat and even the southern flank of our eastern front will look alarmingly at risk.'[32] He was not exaggerating. Taken together, the military developments in the east and in Africa heralded the turn in the tide of the war; the 'Third Reich' was now definitively on the back foot.[33] On 24 November Hitler issued the order to defend the position of the entrapped army in Stalingrad, come what may, and supply it from the air.

In mid-November Goebbels, along with all the other Gauleiters, was appointed a Reich Defence Commissar and thus acquired the power within the 'Reich Defence District' of Berlin to give instructions to the civil authorities. This appointment reinforced his intention to push for 'our conduct of the war to become more radical and more total in every sphere'.[34]

At the end of November he wrote in his diary that 'it's quite clear that in implementing total war we've been guilty of omissions that I have pointed out often enough, though sadly in many cases to no effect. If we had been prompt in introducing and carrying through the conscription of women for work and had combed through the bureaucracy at home, in particular that of the armed forces, the Führer would doubtless have several hundred thousand, if not as many as a million, fresh soldiers to deploy today.' At his next meeting with Hitler he would propose that 'our conduct of the war be radicalized and total-ized in every sphere'. Furthermore: 'If we could decide to put everything into the war, without regard to the front or the home front, then we should easily have people and resources enough at our disposal to cope with the present difficulties.' Privileged circles in the population, however, should no longer be let off lightly, but rather 'everyone must be obliged to participate in the war according to their ability and not according to their inclinations'.[35]

The following day he read in the most recent report from the Security Service, which regularly sounded out the 'mood' in the country, that 'throughout the population' people were asking 'with increasing frequency why we were not introducing total war, for that too was surely the order of the day'.[36] But that was not his only source of information: 'In a secret Security Service report, written for my eyes only, the domestic situation is presented somewhat more critically than in the official report.'

That last diary entry shows that the 'official reports', which to this day are still seen as an important source regarding the attitude of the German population at the time, told the truth only to a limited extent. This was because those who wrote them clearly anticipated possible reactions among their readers within the National Socialist leadership and took that into account when writing. For this and for other methodological reasons it is therefore advisable to read the reports not as an authentic reflection of the 'mood' at the time, but as an important factor that, quite aside from their accuracy, influenced the actions of decision-makers at the time. Goebbels took the following from the special report written for him: 'Here and there voices are heard among the people criticizing the Führer himself, above all because one or other of the Führer's predictions, particularly regarding Stalingrad, has not come true.' Goebbels was not convinced by this interpretation and wanted to attribute it instead to the effect of the season: 'I consider this account to be slightly exaggerated. In my view and in the light of my own experience, confidence in the Führer among the people is completely solid. It's no surprise that there is a certain mood of depression. Since time immemorial November has been the month of depressions.'

Similarly, at the end of November he had 'some worries' about the 'general propaganda situation', for on the whole they were 'somewhat on the defensive':

As far as audiences abroad are concerned, we have nothing concrete to say, in particular regarding plans for the Europe of the future. At home there's rather a lack of a unifying concept for war propaganda over the longer term. I'm striving with every means at my disposal to keep such a concept alive, but it's undermined time and time again by the foolish actions of other departments, sometimes subordinate ones, sounding off prematurely and without my knowledge.

Now, as winter sets in, 'our general propaganda at home and abroad' must regain 'its former powerful persuasive force'. 'Our aims regarding the new Europe' must be set out at the very least 'in rough outline'. 'The absence of concrete military news about the most recent operations' was also beginning 'to look really bad'.[37]

In addition, on this same day he wrote that 'even among those circles that had hitherto resisted this kind of total war' there was a gradual recognition 'that something more has to be done if the war is not to drag on endlessly. Anyone who objects that total war would lead to a certain demoralization of the nation must be reminded that nothing demoralizes people more than a lengthy war. We must therefore try hard to ensure that we win as soon as possible and that gaining time is viewed as the greatest gain of this war.'

Thus the transition from the sense of triumph in the summer to the winter crisis of 1942/3 took place in several phases: In August and September Hitler and those around him were overoptimistic about Germany's ability to achieve the ambitious goals of the summer offensive in the southern part of the eastern front, namely to capture Stalingrad and then advance to Baku and Krasny. Hitler was already daydreaming of being able to use these conquests as the basis for a further advance into the Near East and, combining it with an advance by Rommel against British forces, to encircle Egypt, Palestine, Jordan, and Syria in a pincer movement.

In late October and early November, however, the mood became more sober. The German offensive ground to a halt in the ruins of Stalingrad, on 2 November at the Battle of El-Alamein Montgomery achieved the decisive breakthrough forcing Rommel onto the defensive, and on 8 November American and British forces landed in Algeria and Morocco in the rear of the Axis powers' Africa Army.

Having spoken against exaggerated optimism in war propaganda back in September and having made efforts in October 1942 to steer it in a 'more realistic' direction, Goebbels recognized that the worsening situation in the late autumn might provide an opportunity to intensify propaganda, priming the home population for a tougher line, for the mobilization of all reserves, and for a reduction of those private comforts that still existed.

This possibility became a certainty when on 23 November 1942 the German troops were trapped at Stalingrad and during December more bad news kept coming from the encircled city.

Goebbels's 'Jewish policy' in December 1942

The National Socialist version of 'total war' was not simply a matter of exploiting and mobilizing fully the war potential in every area of life— not only in Germany but also in the occupied territories. Nor was it simply the radicalization of the war itself, which broadly abolished the distinction between combatants and civilians. Rather it also specifically included a racially motivated policy of annihilation. The mass murder of Jews had begun with the invasion of the Soviet Union in the summer of 1941. During the following months, as it were in the shadow of an expanding war whose end seemed to be stretching further and further into the future, it had spread over an ever-growing area and become increasingly intense. Now at the end of 1942 Goebbels set about placing this policy of annihilation openly in the service of a truly 'total' conception of war.

By this stage the systematic murder of the European Jews was far advanced. Those Jews the Germans encountered in the Soviet territories had for the most part already been shot; in Poland the clearance of the ghettos and deportations to extermination camps were in full swing; the deportation trains from the 'Greater German Reich', from France, the Netherlands, and Belgium, were heading for Auschwitz, Majdanek, and the death camps of 'Operation Reinhardt'. A large proportion of Slovakian Jews had also met the same fate by the time deportations from there ceased in October, and by the end of the year the machinery of death had even reached the tiny Jewish community in Norway.

In view of its scale, the crime of the century could not really be kept secret. The deportations from German towns and cities and the subsequent auctions of the household possessions of deportees took place in public and the propaganda machine's eloquent silence about the fate of those deportees caused many to assume the worst. Thus within the 'Greater German Reich' rumours and information about the murder of the Jews were widespread: Among the sources were soldiers and relatives of the occupation administration, who were in a position to report on the shootings in the east, employees of the Reich railways, who drove and administered the deportation trains, or even Germans from the 'Old Reich' who were working temporarily in the Auschwitz area and able to make their own observations.[38]

German propaganda and leading representatives of the regime in particular reacted to this situation by sending out clear signals that essentially confirmed the rumours but did not give any details about the process of murder. Thus in the course of 1942, for example, Hitler mentioned the ongoing 'extermination' of the Jews on several occasions,[39] and in October 1942 the Party Chancellery sent a circular to the Gauleiters and District Leaders commenting on rumours about 'very severe measures against the Jews in the Eastern Territories' in a way that could be interpreted as confirmation.[40]

By the end of 1942 evidence of the mass murder of Jews emerging from European countries under German control was coalescing into an overall picture and being reported increasingly frequently in the media in Allied and neutral states.[41] On 17 December the British Foreign Secretary Anthony Eden read out a declaration from the Allied governments to the UK Parliament accusing the Germans of systematically deporting Jews from across Europe to occupied Poland and of having already murdered hundreds of thousands of them. This declaration was accompanied by press publications, radio broadcasts, and protest demonstrations.[42]

As Propaganda Minister Goebbels was increasingly concerned by the ensuing alarm expressed by the public sphere world-wide. On 5 December 1942 he recorded in his diary the global protests against the 'alleged atrocities committed by the German government against the European Jews'. The next day he rejected a proposal put to him to 'liquidate Jewish marriages', fearing that it would 'create so much disquiet and confusion in public opinion'. Three days later he reacted with consternation: 'The Jews are mobilizing against us across the whole world. They are reporting dreadful atrocities against the Jewish race that we are allegedly guilty of in Poland, and are now threatening via London and Washington to make everyone who has participated in them answer to a fearful criminal court after the war. That cannot prevent us from applying a radical solution to the Jewish question.'[43]

Goebbels finally felt obliged to state his position regarding this matter at his ministry's internal briefing.[44] First of all, on 8 December he issued the instruction to ignore the accusations, though without denying them to his colleagues: 'Regardless of whether there is any truth in these reports, this is rather a sensitive subject and we should steer clear of it, as after a while the enemy will drop this polemic anyway.' 'Ignore' was the subsequent instruction given to the German press.

The next day at the briefing he gave vent to his annoyance at protests by Swedish students at German persecution of the Jews and on 11 December issued the instruction: 'Reports about the oppression of the Polish state and the extermination of the Jews' should be met with 'absolute' silence.

On 12 December he felt compelled to change course and initiate a propaganda counterattack, for he had come to the conclusion that it was impossible 'to deal with this matter in the long run by hushing it up'. In doing so, he conceded to his colleagues that as far as the central issue was concerned there was nothing to deny. In view of the fact that 'hostile news about alleged German atrocities against Jews and Poles is becoming overwhelming and the truth of the matter is that we have little to show in the way of counterevidence', his instruction was 'that we should start using atrocities as propaganda and report in the strongest terms on English atrocities in India, the Near East, Iran, Egypt, and so on—everywhere where the English are based'. This, he claimed, would be a way of 'forcing the English onto the defensive'. He was, incidentally, relying, he said, on the inventiveness of his colleagues for concrete information about British 'atrocities'. When his state secretary Leopold Gutterer objected that photos from the eastern front were often sent home to Germany 'showing Jews and others hanging from gallows', Goebbels got into his stride and commanded that an 'educational pamphlet' should be published 'for the troops', demonstrating the 'criminal activity of the Jews' and clearly stating: 'Either we string up the Jews who are undermining our war effort, or one day the Jews will string us up.' It was, however, 'foolish to photograph such things and send them home' because at home they gave rise to 'inappropriate sentimental responses' and fuelled enemy propaganda.

Although no pamphlet of this kind was in the end produced, Goebbels's comments clearly show that he was prepared to treat this sensitive subject much more openly, at least among eastern front soldiers, who in many cases were eyewitnesses to the murder of Jews. On 13 and 14 December he once again dealt with this topic in his diary entries and concluded coolly with the statement: 'But all this is no use to the Jews. The Jewish race paved the way for this war. It is the spiritual author of all the misery that has befallen the world. Jewry must pay for its crime, just as the Führer prophesied in his speech to the Reichstag: with the elimination of the Jewish race in Europe and perhaps in the entire world.'

On the same day that Goebbels committed these words to paper he again spoke at some length at the ministerial briefing about the 'campaign of exculpation' that was to divert attention from German crimes. In the course of his remarks he once again confirmed that the Allies' accusations did hit the nail on the head, and indeed with disarming candour he even conceded that the figures quoted were accurate in terms of scale: 'We cannot respond to these things; if the Jews say we shot 2½ million Jews in Poland or deported them to the east, of course we can't answer that it was only about 2.3 million. In other words, we're not in a position to engage in an argument—at least not before the eyes of the world.' And he went on: 'In addition, the world is not yet so well informed about the Jewish question for us to dare to say: "Yes indeed, we have done that and for the following reasons." Nobody would even listen to us.'[45]

At the same meeting Goebbels composed further guidelines for the 'campaign of exculpation'. All reports, 'whether from the Near East, from Iran, Palestine, French North Africa, or the East Indies, must now be sensationalized.... For every day of this campaign something new must be invented....' The campaign was not simply to be aimed at foreign propaganda but also at the German media. In the Propaganda Minister's estimation, the Allies' information about German persecution of the Jews had already spread to such an extent within Germany that it required a response.

The 'offensive campaign to resist the enemy's atrocities campaign', Goebbels said two days later, should 'not be limited to the English. We must now strike up a general outcry about atrocities, in which the agitation aimed at us is completely drowned out.'

The press was duly instructed and a series of articles did in fact appear responding to these 'pointers' but there was no broadly based campaign, much to the annoyance of Goebbels, who was constantly warning the press to keep up the pressure. Evidently German journalists lacked the imagination required constantly to come up with new British atrocities in India, Africa, or wherever else, while the situation on the eastern front, the main focus of interest for the reading public in late 1942, was so threatening.

The instruction issued at the press briefing of 22 December, 'Stories of atrocities originating in Moscow and England should not be published' and 'if they are, then only with an extremely aggressive response', indicates how far by the end of the year German propaganda regarding the 'Jewish question' had been put on the defensive. Now some response had to be made to the substance of the Allied accusations.

Thus Goebbels's propaganda strategy during these weeks of not denying the Allies' exposure of the systematic murder of the Jews, but rather of ignoring it or conducting a campaign of diverting attention from it, had failed. As Goebbels could not prevent the spread of information about these crimes—whether it was spread by Allied propaganda, by German soldiers on the eastern front, or by the many Germans who witnessed the deportations—he seems to have made the decision to go on the offensive in dealing with this subject. In concrete terms that meant confirming the rumours circulating about the murders by means of certain signals and hints and making it clear to the Germans that they had long since become witnesses to and complicit in a massive crime and were now faced with the alternative he had mentioned on 12 December: 'Either we string the Jews up or one day the Jews will string us up.' This scenario was to become integral to his efforts to bring in 'total war' and can be explicitly traced in his speech at the Sports Palace.

A dangerous Christmas mood

At the end of the year Goebbels was continuing to follow closely the fate of the 6th Army encircled in Stalingrad. At first, however, his diary entries do not suggest that he was expecting a military catastrophe.[46]

There was very little official reporting about the situation in the east. The fact that the army at Stalingrad was surrounded was still being kept secret and there was a general reluctance to refer to German positions using place names. Based on reports on the national mood, Goebbels concluded that the German population was becoming increasingly anxious. The average citizen also remained largely in the dark about the true situation in Africa. Goebbels blamed the Wehrmacht High Command (OKW) for this, for it was responsible for issuing the daily Wehrmacht reports.[47]

Shortly before Christmas, however, he reached the conclusion himself on the strength of the military information accessible to him that the 'situation in the east' as a whole was 'critical'.[48] Christmas to his mind was psychologically unsettling because it encouraged reflection: Though, as in previous years, he instructed the media to hold back on

Christmas-related material, he nevertheless noted resignedly that 'a Christmas mood arises simply because Christmas is coming'.[49] Then he made fresh attempts to suppress his own worries: 'In my view things will sort themselves out sooner or later. We must learn from last winter's crisis about what we have to do. Up to now the bolshevists have never achieved a significant operational success, and they won't this winter either.'[50]

In order to counteract the Christmas mood, he deliberately began devising a National Socialist alternative to the Christian notion of resurrection. At the end of the year he published an article in *Das Reich* in which his aim, as he put it in his diary, was to consider the 'problem of our fallen servicemen... from a higher vantage point'. In the article he writes that those who die young in war seem to him to be 'the complete ones': 'When they took their leave of life it embraced them with its heroic rhythm. The great goal we must fight and labour for through difficult days and sleepless, watchful nights has already stretched out its hand to them in the final minute of their earthly life.' And: 'Our dead are already standing on life's other shore in its blazing light. We are searching, while they are complete. They have fulfilled their time early, whereas it still lies before us with its multitude of problems and obligations.'[51]

Planning for 'total war' begins

On 28 December Martin Bormann, the powerful head of the Party Chancellery and Hitler's close confidant, visited Goebbels on behalf of the 'Führer' to discuss plans for the ceremony to mark the tenth anniversary of the seizure of power on 30 January.[52] According to Bormann, this was not to be an occasion for 'trumpeting future projects but for giving an account' of themselves. This was a formulation directed against the plans of Robert Ley, head of the German Labour Front (DAF), to have Hitler announce far-reaching social legislation. Ley had already attempted to gain Goebbels's support for these plans.[53] In addition, as Goebbels recorded in his diary, Hitler had given Bormann the task of 'talking through with me the issue of total war in all its aspects'. Goebbels saw this as a 'real triumph', as 'all the ideas and proposals I have put forward repeatedly for a year and a half are now to be realised in one fell swoop'.

Goebbels began the new year by putting all his energies into his project of 'total war'. For him three things were essential: the introduction of compulsory work for women, the suspension of industries not essential to the war effort, and the closure of expensive nightclubs and restaurants and of luxury stores.[54] In the ministry he gave instructions for a detailed 'memorandum on total warfare' to be compiled. Its tone, in line with his own thinking, was highly interventionist and the memorandum was sent on his orders to the head of the Reich Chancellery Hans-Heinrich Lammers.[55] At the very beginning of January Goebbels had discussions with various individuals,[56] committed his colleagues to his course of action at the ministerial briefing,[57] and in his diary reiterated his belief that the 'totalization' of the war was the key to victory.[58]

Then, as he had hoped, on 8 January a small group gathered for a crucial meeting, which he chaired. The other participants were Lammers, Bormann, Wilhelm Keitel, head of the Wehrmacht High Command, the Minister for the Economy Walther Funk, Fritz Sauckel, the 'Reich Commissioner for Labour', as well as Albert Speer, Reich Minister for Armaments and Munitions.[59]

After Keitel had outlined the shortage of men in the Wehrmacht, Goebbels intervened, elucidating the 'whole matter at some length from a political perspective'. From the start he adopted a radical tone, attacking 'any indulgence in illusions' and (in line with the motto 'Nothing is impossible') giving examples from the 'time of struggle'. In concrete terms his demands amounted to 'our presenting the Führer within a relatively short time with 500,000 men hitherto classed as exempted from war service'. Hitler had asked Speer to provide an additional 200,000 men 'from the munitions sector for the front'. Sauckel raised a few objections, believing he could solve the problem with the resources he already had, namely above all by acquiring more foreign slave labour. However, in the ensuing discussion Goebbels succeeded in overcoming these objections with the support of Funk, Speer, and Bormann.

Finally, they agreed on the wording of a Führer decree. During the following days, Sauckel created a few more difficulties, but eventually a draft accepted by all the participants was presented to Hitler.[60]

After this initial success Goebbels launched a propaganda offensive, in part to put pressure on those colleagues who were still hesitating and in part to fill the propaganda vacuum that was in danger of arising from Hitler's stubborn silence in the face of the developing crisis.

On 17 January in *Das Reich* he published under the heading 'Total War' a programmatic article, the central proposition of which was: 'The more radical and total we are in our methods of waging war, the sooner we shall achieve final victory.' A 'certain small section of our nation', he said, seemed to think that was none of its business, and accordingly he directed his polemic against 'slackers', 'idlers', and 'parasites'.[61]

Although he was forced to admit in his diary that discussing such topics was 'somewhat detrimental' to foreign propaganda, the 'political advantages at home' in his view outweighed this concern.[62]

The following week he therefore pressed on and expressed his thoughts more concretely under the heading 'The Optics of the War'—a key term that he would use again in his Sports Palace speech on 18 February: The 'external appearance of the war at home', he wrote, was 'by no means such that anyone can tell at first glance that it is make-or-break time'. What was to be done? The 'maintenance of our cultural life', radio, theatre, film, went without question. But shops that had nothing left to sell, bars, gourmet restaurants and the like would have to close.[63]

The Führer decree, signed eventually by Hitler on 13 January, concerning the comprehensive plan to use men and women for tasks relating to the defence of the Reich was broadly in line with Goebbels's ideas. In particular, it envisaged extensive economic restructuring to free up all the labour that could be used in the armaments industry and in the Wehrmacht. To this end, all types of work that hitherto had been classed as 'reserved occupations' were to be reviewed, anyone not yet engaged in officially recognized 'work' was to be registered, and businesses not vital to the war effort were to be shut down.[64]

To carry out these tasks Hitler created a 'Committee of Three' consisting of Keitel, Lammers, and Bormann to report to him regularly. Originally Goebbels took it as read that that he would also be a member of this committee,[65] but was forced to accept Keitel taking his place. His only consolation was the phrase in the decree that talked of the committee 'liaising closely' with him.

Only a few days after Hitler had signed, however, Goebbels recorded the first adverse reactions: 'Certain circles are doing their utmost to exclude me from the inner advisory committee.... I am very worried that Lammers and Keitel in particular will attempt to water down the most radical decisions.'[66] The inclusion of Bormann nevertheless persuaded him that he had succeeded in ensuring that 'my own work is set out in precise detail in the Committee of Three and enjoys the greatest influence. There is, in other words, no danger that I can be overridden in an unguarded moment.'[67]

On 20 January 1943 Goebbels took part in the first meeting of the 'Committee of Four' as he self-confidently named it; apart from him, a number of specialist advisers and also Sauckel and Funk had been included.

In discussions with Lammers and Bormann, Goebbels concluded that his position in the committee had been established once and for all: 'I am regarded as and acknowledged to be the driving force in the whole project, and besides that all suggestions I make regarding new decrees and the revision of previous decrees are simply waved through.'[68] In particular, he had succeeded in 'overcoming all bureaucratic reservations and objections' concerning the prospective 'general work requirement, even for women,' and in 'bringing about a radical decision'. In retrospect this turned out to be a somewhat premature conclusion to draw.

In view of the population's increasing anxiety about the Reich's military situation such drastic measures in the civilian sector seemed to Goebbels particularly urgent. In the first half of January he had gauged the 'mood'—contrary to his own pronouncements he still held to this concept—as still relatively positive.[69] A few days later he certainly still regarded 'bearing and mood' as 'calm and assured',[70] but by the middle of the month the situation began to change dramatically.[71]

Concerns were now focused on the eastern front and in particular on the fate of the 6th Army, which had been encircled in Stalingrad for almost eight weeks. On 16 January it was felt that the OKW's official daily report[72] must finally admit this. The fact, however, that in the following days propaganda contained suspiciously little about the fate of the trapped army inevitably caused significant anxiety.[73] Goebbels's diaries also show that during this period the reports on the military situation to which he had access led him to take an increasingly pessimistic view of Stalingrad, which according to his entry for 21 January was finally becoming 'catastrophic'.[74]

In the light of this, Goebbels's campaign for 'total war' was designed not only to intensify the war effort, provide more men for the armed forces, and ramp up munitions production, he was also hoping that the adjustment in public life to the austerity of war would bring about a certain psychological relief, distracting people from the crisis and providing a sort of therapy through activity. At the same time, however, the regime's reach was to be extended. Mobilization for 'total war' was intended to strengthen the authority of Party and state and increase their control over the population. The collection of woollen garments the previous year provided a model: During the winter crisis of 1941/2 the regime had attempted to counteract the mood of despair by mounting a campaign across the whole nation linking the 'homeland' with the 'front'.[75] If the population was completely taken up with the harsh realities of war it would display a strengthened moral 'bearing' that would override fluctuations in mood. 'The call for total war is becoming louder week by week', Goebbels suggested in his diary.[76]

The predictable catastrophe of the 6th Army at Stalingrad made swift action seem a matter of urgency. 'We must now gradually get used to the idea', as Goebbels wrote on 21 January, 'of letting the German nation know about the situation there'. In fact, this could have happened long before then, but up to that point, he writes, Hitler had always opposed it. Now they could wait no longer. 'For us Stalingrad must become what the Alcazar was in the fight for Spanish freedom: an epic tale of German soldiers' heroism, more moving and tragic than anything one could make up.'

Hitler's order

On the evening of 21 January Goebbels made the journey to Hitler's East Prussian headquarters for a crucial interview. There, as he noted the following day, in view of the general situation the 'mood was rather despondent and extraordinarily serious'.[77] In this atmosphere he was to be successful (at least by his own estimation) in gaining Hitler's acceptance for his wide-ranging plan of action for 'total war', the dictator being in a depressed and maudlin frame of mind.

Goebbels's very detailed report on this visit also shows how concerned he was to impress his ideas on leading figures close to Hitler in the secluded setting of the headquarters. Thus, after a number of individual discussions before his meeting with Hitler, he had concluded that 'my preparatory work towards total war has already put down deep roots'.

Rudolf Schmundt, Hitler's Wehrmacht adjutant, encouraged him in his intention of giving Hitler 'a no-holds-barred account of what's on my heart and he promised, if push came to shove, to ensure that the entire Wehrmacht would back me up.' Hitler's adjutant Albert Bormann (Martin's brother) and Karl Brandt, Hitler's personal physician, also supported Goebbels's approach.

After this first round of talks he finally met with Hitler, who asked him to accompany him on a morning walk round the headquarters site. 'The Führer described to me the situation in Stalingrad, which is simply desperate. Some 200,000 men are, after all, trapped there, without the slightest hope that we can relieve them.' The catastrophe, as Hitler went on, had been caused first and foremost 'by the complete failure of our allies'. At first Goebbels listened patiently but then took advantage of the walk to present his ideas about moving to total war. With success: 'I can see from my first attempt that I shall have no problem with the Führer.'

But first Hitler went off to his daily briefing meeting, while Goebbels discussed the 'present press situation' with Reich Press Chief Dietrich, focusing again on his key idea of winning acceptance for a harder line: 'The press has to adopt a completely different tone from hitherto. We can no longer treat the population in such a gentle, bourgeois way. Instead of just pursing our lips, we must now start to whistle.'

Dietrich understood and immediately formulated a 'watchword of the day', which briefed the press on the new tasks ahead. The 'heroic and moving sacrifice', he wrote, 'that the encircled German troops at Stalingrad are offering the German nation, taken together with the imminent requirement for women to work, and other radical organizational measures necessary for total war, will become the moral force behind a truly heroic stance on the part of the German people and the starting point marking a new determination to achieve victory and redouble all our efforts'.[78]

Later that day Goebbels met General Zeitzler, the new army Chief of the General Staff. In the latter's opinion, Goebbels alone could have a decisive impact on the war: 'I was the only person, he said, who could tell the Führer everything calmly and objectively, who enjoyed his full confidence, and about whose integrity as a National Socialist he had no doubts.' Even Karl Wolff, Himmler's liaison officer with Hitler, assured him of the Reichsführer SS's total support.

Finally, at lunchtime Goebbels was once more alone with Hitler. The dictator again launched into a lament: Germany's allies were unreliable and had failed, the air force leadership had not fulfilled its promises. They were deep in discussion when, as if arranged by Goebbels, a phone call from Zeitzler came informing Hitler of the Red Army's critical incursion into the German positions at Stalingrad. The desired effect on Hitler followed immediately: 'This news has profoundly shocked the Führer.' Hitler's response to the news showed that he was beginning to realize he must abandon hope of 'keeping' at least 'some kind of combat force in Stalingrad', which might in the right circumstances be relieved later.

Goebbels made use of the situation to present to Hitler his 'reorganization programme for the home front': the introduction of compulsory work for women, the 'dissolving of all organizations and enterprises not important or necessary to the war effort' and the 'complete gearing of all aspects of civilian life at home to the needs of the war'.

He was resoundingly successful: 'From the outset the Führer approves everything I put to him. He makes no difficulties at all; on the contrary, on several points he goes even further than I have suggested.' The dictator did not, however, permit Goebbels to become a member of the Committee of Three; clearly Hitler feared that if too many leading politicians were involved then a sort of war cabinet, a real power centre, might emerge, and if Hitler knew how to prevent anything it was the creation of bodies that might limit his powers. Goebbels's exclusion was explained on the grounds that 'he should not be burdened by the administration of this great programme'. Rather, he was to 'act in this great enterprise like a constantly running engine', continuously overseeing and monitoring the committee's work, for which task Hitler assured him of his full support. Goebbels was admittedly forced to concede that Hitler's decree of 13 January was again significantly watered down by the lowering of the upper age limit for women's compulsory work from fifty to forty-five.[79]

Finally, the dictator and his propaganda minister met at ten in the evening for a final round of talks lasting until 3.30 in the morning. Hitler approved additional proposals from Goebbels for 'total war', such that Goebbels at last felt he had secured what he wanted: 'A sort of internal dictatorship is being set up through the appointment of these four men and I am supposed to be the psychological dictator and the motor for the whole initiative.' Almost in the same breath the men turned to the 'Jewish question in Berlin', for which the 'speediest' solution had to be found: 'While there are still Jews in Berlin, there can be no talk of internal security. The Jews of Vienna must also be expelled as soon as possible.'

The conversation then ranged over several other topics. After discussing a variety of personnel matters, they eventually exchanged views on art and philosophy. Then Speer joined them and they spent several hours by the fire in Hitler's study. As a result of the bad news from Stalingrad the mood was 'melancholy'.

Goebbels left the headquarters in the dead of night: 'I have achieved everything I set out to achieve and more. I believe that the decisions taken on this crucial Friday will very possibly bring about a decisive turn in the war.' The next day he committed to paper his account of the discussions. It ran to ninety pages.[80]

Initial resistance

Bormann was the first person he telephoned about his discussion with Hitler. He formed with him a 'dual alliance with the aim of setting about the work in the most radical fashion, sparing no one and nothing, and fulfilling the single task of providing the front with the men needed'.[81] At the morning ministry briefing Goebbels made it clear 'that the Propaganda Ministry and my staff will be particularly involved in introducing and carrying out the radicalization of our entire war effort. Just as in the second half of 1932 I with my staff were responsible for the essential themes of our revolution's propaganda, now in the crisis of this war we shall do the same again.'[82]

Strong resistance to the 'totalization of our war effort at home' was, however, quickly in evidence from a variety of quarters and was directed in particular against the closure of businesses and compulsory work for women.[83] Goebbels was faced with Göring pressurizing him to preserve luxury restaurants and exclusive shops in Berlin.[84] He also suspected that Lammers was undermining compulsory work for women by insisting on exemptions for mothers, even in cases where childcare was not an issue. Thereupon Goebbels began to regard Lammers as the centre of resistance to his more radical approach: 'He sees the whole business more from a complacent bourgeois point of view. Now, however, it will no longer do to set about this or that problem in a leisurely way or simply to mark time. We have to make fundamental changes.'[85]

At the end of January Goebbels took part in a further meeting of the 'Committee of Four', which in his view had been 'extraordinarily heated'. Whereas he along with Speer supported a 'fairly radical proposal' from Funk to close down businesses, Lammers, backed up by Bormann and Sauckel, held out against it. According to Goebbels, Lammers was 'not reliable': 'Wherever he can, he torpedoes radical decisions.' Although Lammers and Bormann could refer expressly to a 'Führer decision' not to cause unnecessary unemployment as a result of the closures, Goebbels was convinced that he could reverse this decision by speaking personally to the Führer. If Goebbels created the impression in his diary that at the meeting measures had been taken to provide the armaments industry with 300,000 additional people, then he clearly misjudged the situation, as the meagre results of the initiative show. He was simply unwilling to admit to himself that it was not only in the case of compulsory work for women that Hitler shrank from lending his authority to radical but possibly unpopular measures.[86]

The day before the meeting Goebbels had written a further article on the subject of 'total war' that was to appear in Das Reich on 7 February. 'If I come up against serious difficulties in the Committee of Four, I intend to take refuge more in the public sphere', as he explained his tactics in his diary. 'Public opinion is always a good ally.'[87] In an article entitled 'A Tough Lesson' he prepared his readers for the more uncompromising course to be taken in politics at home: 'Many of us fail to accept this adjustment at home because they still think in concepts and categories that belong to the past and have been superseded. They cannot imagine living a life appropriate to wartime. They consider things that are part of modern civilization to be indispensable, when these things were unknown twenty years ago, let alone a hundred years ago. They would quickly be forced to give up not only these things but quite a few more if we did not have the strength to bring the war to a victorious conclusion.'[88]

Dress rehearsal: Goebbels's speech at the Sports Palace on 30 January 1943

During preparations for the celebration of the tenth anniversary of the seizure of power on 30 January 1943 Goebbels had managed to persuade Hitler to shorten significantly the lengthy programme that had been originally planned.[89] As Hitler continued to avoid public appearances with defeat at Stalingrad imminent, it fell to Goebbels to read out a proclamation from Hitler at the Berlin Sports Palace and to use the occasion to make a keynote speech.[90]

In addition to the impending catastrophe at Stalingrad, while preparing for this speech Goebbels was faced with another challenge. On 26 January the *Völkische Beobachter* (along with other press organs[91]) reported that Churchill, 'according to reliable reports', had gone to Washington a few days earlier.[92] In fact, however, the conference held by Roosevelt and Churchill had concluded two days before in Casablanca, Morocco. Goebbels's diary indicates that at this point he too was still assuming it had taken place in Washington.[93]

On 26 January the British and Americans published a very non-specific communiqué about the meeting. Two days later a derogatory commentary ('empty communiqué and a bit of theatre for the cameras'[94]) entitled 'The Casablanca Film' (the Bogart film was showing just at that time in the USA) appeared in the *Völkische Beobachter*; the other print media also adopted an ostentatiously indifferent attitude. Nevertheless, the reporting in the *Völkische Beobachter* (and other newspapers) revealed that the Allies had managed to mislead the Germans totally about the location of the conference. Goebbels made the resigned comment in his diary that his own news service had 'once again failed completely'.[95] Had they perhaps translated indications of the location of the conference literally as 'The White House' and drawn erroneous conclusions from that? This very public embarrassment was in itself a good reason to make only passing reference to the conference in the German media.

In addition, the main problem for German propaganda was that it had not the slightest knowledge of the content of the ten days of discussions between the USA and Britain about their future joint military strategy. Goebbels therefore issued the guideline that propaganda should claim that serious differences between the Allies and their difficulties in combating German U boats were the reason for the conference.[96]

The demand, made in Casablanca by Roosevelt in particular and contained in the joint communiqué, for unconditional surrender on the part of Germany, Japan, and Italy was not reported by the *Völkische Beobachter* or by any other leading newspaper,[97] even though at his ministerial briefing Goebbels had insisted that the German people should be informed.[98] It was only in his diary that he commented on the capitulation demand as illusory.[99] He evidently regarded it as a tactical mistake to go into the matter further and thus enable the Western Allies to control the narrative on yet another topic and put German propaganda under pressure. Yet because he had to assume that foreign radio broadcasts would make the demand for capitulation common knowledge among the German home population, he did devote one sentence to it in his 30 January speech, though without giving any details about Casablanca. 'We have always held to the firm and unalterable principle', he proclaimed, 'that in our vocabulary the word "capitulation" does not exist'.[100]

Goebbels may well have quickly realized that his convoluted treatment of the dangerous c-word was apt to make him sound defensive. He therefore avoided referring to it in future. Engaging publicly with the Allies on the subject of how the war might possibly end was simply incompatible with the campaign he was waging for a heroic mobilization of the nation's last reserves; Casablanca and the demand for unconditional surrender would not be mentioned in his second Sports Palace speech on 18 February. Even on 30 January he concentrated instead on the big topic he had been preparing for months.

Goebbels now took advantage of the opportunity of introducing Hitler's proclamation of 30 January with a speech of his own to further his own agenda. In his forty-five-minute address he tried out some of the key topics of 18 February and gauged their resonance with his audience and with the leadership.

First of all, Goebbels invoked the special aura that the Sports Palace had for Berlin National Socialists as the 'battleground of the movement' (I will come back to the history of this link later on). Here in years past, he said, they had together experienced 'all the highs and lows of Germany's political development and, in wartime, its military development', but here too 'the crucial decisions' needed to combat threats had been proclaimed 'to the whole nation'. 'From this podium the inspiring political watchwords went out and still go out to the nation, uniting it in a fanatical determination to fight.'

Having opened up a route to the topic of the current situation, he left his audience in no doubt about the seriousness of their position: 'The fight for our lives is approaching its dramatic climax.' They were, he said, involved in 'a gigantic contest for the future fate of Europe, indeed of western civilization as a whole'. He denounced in particular the real opponent, as he saw it, lurking behind the unnatural enemy alliance of 'bolshevism and plutocracy': 'International Jewry, which, as so often, once again believes it can triumph over us, but has reckoned without us.' However, the most recent military setbacks in this historic struggle were (and here Goebbels was paving the way for his actual appeal) 'merely an alarm bell alerting us to the need for total war and we are absolutely determined to pursue it'. He wanted, he said, only to 'confirm an established fact', namely: 'The German nation is totally prepared to concentrate all its strength.' And he declared: 'Throughout our nation the cry for the most total war effort in the broadest sense of the word is making itself heard.' He repeated this central message of his speech, the claim that the nation itself was demanding 'total', indeed 'the most total' war, only a few minutes later in almost identical terms.

The audience reacted particularly vigorously to his anti-Semitic attacks but above all also to the passages in his speech calling on people to give up 'all comfortable bourgeois habits', thereby playing on feelings of resentment against the 'better off': 'Whether you're of high rank or low [loud applause], whether you're rich or poor [more loud applause] in this life-and-death struggle of the German nation no one can be exempt from putting all their strength and everything they possess at the disposal of the fatherland.'

Afterwards Goebbels considered the speech to have had a 'tremendous' impact; he felt the 'tumultuous applause' and the 'impassioned interjections' amounted to a plebiscite on his 'efforts to make the war more total': 'In other words, as far as the people are concerned, my views are not only not too radical, they're not nearly radical enough. At the moment it's impossible to push too hard.'[101]

He regarded the response of a group of top NS functionaries present as particularly worthy of note. Among them were Robert Ley, leader of the German Labour Front, Konstantin Hierl, Reich Labour Service Leader, and the Reichsführer SS Heinrich Himmler, who 'after five minutes were completely at one with the audience'. The conclusion of the rally reminded him 'of the best times from the period of struggle'. The excitement in the auditorium had been such that an air-raid warning that had sounded during the rally had been completely ignored. That night he received a phone call from Hitler, who had listened to the speech on the radio and spoke of it with 'great enthusiasm'.[102]

Shortly afterwards Goebbels was able to infer from the mood reports he had received that the rally had to a considerable degree 'counteracted' the negative mood, even if many people had expressed a wish for more details about the impending measures.[103] For Goebbels one thing was of overriding importance: 'More than anything, the thunderous applause after I announced radical and total war measures has caused an immense stir throughout the nation.'[104] The nation, as he inferred from the reports, wanted 'total war ... as soon as possible, for the measures taken hitherto have been too ineffectual, and to some extent confidence in the leadership, indeed in the Führer himself, has been dented because the setbacks we have suffered have not led people to draw the appropriate conclusions.'[105] In his view Goebbels had therefore passed the test and he was to make use of a number of experiences from this event in his speech of 18 February.

This attempt to provide a substitute for the speech Hitler himself usually made every 30 January—a speech the public also expected—in the form of a proclamation read out by Goebbels followed by his own speech clearly revealed the propaganda machine's difficulties in the face of Hitler's silence during the most serious crisis the Nazi state had experienced since 1933. The regime was in fact reliant on documenting public consent for the Führer's policies through a regular sequence of large-scale events. If these did not take place the system was in danger of losing its linchpin and simply drifting, which made a leadership crisis seem inevitable. Thus, in Goebbels's view as propaganda expert, extraordinary efforts were needed to maintain the idea of the Führer state without a visible Führer.

The catastrophe at Stalingrad

At the end of January 1943 the propaganda machine set about preparing the population for the 6th Army's devastating defeat. The emotionally charged language of the daily headlines in the *Völkische Beobachter* ('Heroic Resistance' (24 January), 'Undying Honour' (25 January), 'Everlasting Glory' (29 January)) indicated clearly that the end was imminent. By now the pocket had split into two halves, the southern part surrendering on 31 January, while resistance in the north collapsed two days later.[106]

The fact that the Commander in Chief of the 6th Army, Friedrich Paulus, who on 31 January had been promoted to the rank of Field Marshal, allowed himself to be taken prisoner along with a number of other generals was felt by Goebbels to be 'far from gratifying'. Like Hitler he had assumed that in defeat Paulus had no other option than an 'honourable soldier's death'. By surviving, however, the general represented an 'irreparable loss of prestige' in the light of the 'extraordinarily heavy sacrifices' of men and officers.[107] Goebbels was thus forced to engage with Soviet propaganda, which was doing all it could 'to bring home to German troops and the German people that their generals had gone into captivity while the soldiers had been forced to die'.[108]

Be that as it may, Goebbels was forced to deal with how to frame the special announcement about the impending fall of Stalingrad. He opted for a tone designed to be 'very realistic, very sober and emotionally restrained'; he was able to gain Hitler's agreement that there should be three days of remembrance rather than the seven originally planned.[109] At four in the afternoon on 3 February the loss of the city and of the 6th Army was finally announced on the radio, the setting being a 'suitably heroic ceremonial' (Goebbels). According to him, the announcement 'sent a kind of shockwave through the German nation'.[110]

Goebbels set out the direction of the propaganda campaign to follow in a leading article he wrote the same day and which appeared ten days later in *Das Reich* under the heading 'Our Will and Our Way'. The 'total war' measures that had been prepared weeks before were to counteract the dismay and depression spreading throughout the population: 'There can be no more talk of our nation wanting to be spared. People know the uncompromising truth and are now clamouring for the equally uncompromising consequences to be drawn. The measures taken thus far are not too severe for them but rather possibly not severe enough.... In a word: total war in every area of life is the order of the day.'[111]

After the disaster: the political leadership's response

On 5 and 6 February, immediately after the fall of Stalingrad, Goebbels took part in a conference of Gauleiters and Reichsleiters in Posen (Poznań). There he gave a presentation on 'matters concerning total war', which in his own estimation met with 'unreserved approval and universal applause.... My sense is that with the Gauleiters I was

running at open doors in what I said.'[112] He did, however, take grave
offence at Sauckel's presentation, for Sauckel as the man responsible for
labour deployment had made it clear that, as far as mobilizing labour
was concerned, his priority was not the deployment of women but
rather the continued supply of foreigners as forced labour.[113] Goebbels
felt obliged to take the floor again after Sauckel 'in order to make up
for what he omitted'.[114] Contrary to the impression Goebbels sought
to convey in his diaries (Sauckel had, he claims, received only 'very
half-hearted applause'), it is altogether likely that Sauckel, with his
cautious approach to the deployment of women, had the Gauleiters'
support more than Goebbels had with his radical rhetoric.

After their conference in Posen the Gauleiters and Reichsleiters met
on 7 February at the Führer headquarters at Rastenburg, where Hitler
was at pains to explain the current situation to them in a presentation
lasting almost two hours.[115] As Goebbels recorded later in his diary,
Hitler began by invoking the shared experiences of the 'time of
struggle' and maintaining that now 'the means and methods by which
we overcame Party crises in the past' must be used to overcome the
present crisis. He laid the blame for the catastrophe in the east first and
foremost at the door of their allies—the Romanians, the Italians, and
the Hungarians—though he conceded that the Germans had not had
'an accurate enough idea of the vast numbers of people in the east'.

According to Hitler, at the root of the disaster 'was the fact that the
bolshevists had harnessed the nation's strength much more vigorously
than we'. This remark was grist to Goebbels's mill: 'In other words the
Führer confirms my own theory that we have more or less been fighting with one hand tied behind our backs. We've by no means exhausted
our potential and that is why we've had such great difficulties on the
eastern front.'

Hitler dismissed the landing in North Africa as 'a very foolish course
of action', whereas the situation on the eastern front, he claimed, had
in the meantime been almost completely sorted out. Goebbels noted:
'By and large the Führer takes the view that the crisis can be regarded
as more or less over', though their opponents had an important advantage: 'Jewry acts in all enemy states as a driving force, he said, and we
have nothing equally forceful to put up against it. This means we must
eliminate Jewry not only from Reich territory but from the whole of
Europe. In this matter too the Führer and I are of one mind: Berlin
must be first and in the foreseeable future no Jew must be allowed to
remain in Berlin.'

Goebbels was moved by Hitler's announcement that a collapse of the Reich 'would also mean the end of his life.... Should the German nation ever become weak, however, it would deserve nothing other than to be wiped out by a stronger nation; in that case it wouldn't deserve any pity.'

At a further meeting of the Committee of Three on 10 February Goebbels, according to his diary, addressed one of the, in his view, central structural problems of the 'Third Reich', namely 'the difficult problem of demarcating the responsibilities of the individual ministries'. There were, he claimed, 'too many bodies with special powers in the Reich and as a result people are working against one another and this person is trying to poach authority from that person'. It was 'difficult to get the Führer to make clear and firm decisions in this matter; even so, they will be unavoidable in the long run'. At the very least those areas of responsibility that 'positively cry out to be clearly defined' ought to be sorted out.[116] The fact, however, that Hitler made such heavy weather of defining areas of responsibility clearly had its deeper roots in his position of dominance, which rested to a significant extent on a finely balanced relationship of competition and tension among the individual members of the leadership. This sally of Goebbels thus shows clearly that his aim was to bring fundamental change to the entire system of government.

A 'certain terroristic statement': preparations for 18 February 1943

Only two days later, however, Goebbels saw clearly that his efforts to use the Committee of Three to exert a decisive influence on the policies of the regime as a whole had not been very successful. He found it necessary to protest to Bormann that the 'so-called Committee of Three' was making decisions in which he had not been involved.[117] He also addressed the same complaint to the Reich Chancellery. His intervention seems to have had no effect, however, for his formal participation in measures taken by the Committee of Three had not featured in the relevant Führer decree. In the end, therefore, he decided not to take the matter to Hitler.[118]

It now seemed to Goebbels to be all the more necessary to make use of 'the public sphere' in order to achieve his demands. On 9 February he had already noted in his diary that a substitute for the 'not quite

adequate legal foundations' for 'total war' could only be found in
'a certain terroristic statement from the Party that will encompass those
who up to now have been attempting one way or another to avoid
playing their part in the war'.

He was confirmed in this resolve by the large number of letters he
received. In his view they gave clear proof that his initiatives to move
to total war would meet with the nation's 'wholehearted approval'.[119]
He also took the most recent SD report as confirmation of his ideas,
for the larger the problems loomed, the more 'vigorously the masses
demand total war', indeed, people were demanding 'overwhelmingly
that the government introduce not just total war but the most total
war'. People were seeing him more and more 'as the *spiritus rector* of
this whole movement' and, as he believed he could infer from the
reports of the propaganda offices under him, had 'remarkable confidence in me personally and in my active involvement'.[120]

Goebbels was more than willing to deliver. On 13 February he wrote
in his diary that with regard to the 'measures to achieve total war' there
had to be 'more chivvying and pressure' and to 'this end I'm organizing
a new mass rally next Friday in the Sports Palace and I intend again to
make sure plenty of proper old Party comrades are there'. In addition,
as many big-wigs as possible were to be invited in order to witness a
demonstration that 'outdoes in its radicalism anything previously seen'.
The guests of honour would then see 'what's what'.

He would, he said, 'have this rally broadcast over all radio stations in
order also to exert pressure on public opinion in the individual Gaus,
with the result that any Gauleiter who has hitherto been resisting this
or that stringent measure will perhaps fall into line and make up for
lost time for fear of coming under a lot of pressure from public opinion'. And once again Goebbels made use of the familiar comparison:
'We must now once more make use of the tried and tested weapons
from the time before 1933.' As he wrote two days later, he was 'still
there as a motor to drive things forward and I will use the whip until
the sleepyheads have woken up'.[121]

On the actual day of the rally in the Sports Palace the press was
instructed that their 'impressions of the mood' must 'refer to the rally
as a national event and give expression to the fighting resolve of the
whole German nation'. Particular emphasis should be laid on the 'two
cardinal points of the speech..., the anti-bolshevist theme and the
theme of total war'. The 'ten questions that Dr Goebbels will put to

the German people will, however, claim pride of place'.[122] The press was to hark back to 'the language of the time of struggle'.[123]

Significantly, on this same 18 February Goebbels was deeply pre-occupied with the 'Jewish question'. In his diary he records that the Berlin Jews would now 'finally be deported'. As a first step they would be assembled in camps by the end of February and then 'be subject to deportation' in batches of up to 2,000 people daily. Goebbels was clearly determined to give maximum support to this SS operation: 'I have set myself the goal of making Berlin free of Jews by the middle or at the latest by the end of March. I hope and believe that by doing this we shall again greatly ease the psychological situation.'[124]

Also on this day and before his speech he wrote an additional article for *Das Reich* entitled 'The European Crisis' in which he identified those he alleged to be truly responsible for the present state of the war: 'If, however, one takes a good look at the background, international Jewry is quickly revealed as the *spiritus rector* of all this psychological and intellectual confusion, the leaven of decomposition in states and nations.'[125] The article appeared on 28 February, immediately after arrests in Berlin began.

If, as we shall see, Goebbels once more introduced a series of harsh anti-Semitic statements into his speech, ensuring an eager audience response, one purpose of this tactic was to create a receptive psycho-logical attitude among the National Socialists of the Berlin Gau to the imminent deportation of the Berlin Jews. This public propagating of a 'solution' to the 'Jewish question', one that while not disclosed in detail was nevertheless clearly extremely radical, was therefore an inte-gral component of Goebbels's conception of 'total war': The people were to be left in no doubt that through such measures they had burnt their boats and that as a result their only hope of escaping the bloody retribution they feared was to achieve final victory.

Thus Goebbels's speech at the Sports Palace on 18 February repre-sented the climax of a campaign that he had been planning in his own mind in the final months of 1942 and had been actively developing in January 1943, initially within the leadership of the regime. He used his address on 30 January 1943 as a trial run. His speech on 18 February was the apex, as it were, of his sustained efforts to persuade the regime's lead-ers to commit to a more radical policy at home in support of the war effort and to assume himself, as the prime mover in this new course of action, a central role in the conduct of the war on the 'home front'.

2

Goebbels's speech on 'total war'

Text and commentary

Goebbels delivered his speech on 18 February between 5 and 7 pm and it was broadcast on the radio at 8 pm. The listeners were not aware, however, that they were hearing a recording and we cannot be sure that it was not altered before being broadcast: thunderous applause may, for example, have been lengthened or the volume of audience reactions in the venue increased. The text printed here and my commentary on it are based on this recording and not on the printed version that appeared in the press and as a booklet. A comparison shows that a number of changes were made in the printed version, including the addition or deletion of half-sentences or even whole ones. All significant reactions on the part of the audience have been noted. Extracts from the speech were disseminated via newsreel but a complete recording on film seems not to exist.

The venue for the rally, the Sports Palace on Potsdam Street in the Schöneberg district,[1] had played a significant role in the history of the Berlin NSDAP since the first mass rally there in 1928. As 'National Socialism's old battleground' (as the *Völkische Beobachter* called it in its report on 19 February of Goebbels's speech) it symbolized for the Berlin Nazi Party and its members the breathtaking political success achieved by the National Socialists in establishing a mass base.

It was not until 1933, however, that the NSDAP (in other words the leadership of the Berlin Gau, namely Goebbels) possessed de facto sole authority over the use of the building for political events. Throughout the Weimar Republic more or less all the major parties held mass rallies in the Sports Palace. Opened in 1910, this imposing venue had multiple uses. It was over 110 metres long, 54 metres wide, and almost 20 metres high,[2] and the interior had no pillars to block the view. Before and after 1933, it was also used, among other things, for ice sports, revues, cycling competitions, and boxing matches, which lent it the popular appeal that Nazi propaganda then blended with the narrative of the 'old battleground'. Thus for many this was a place with a special aura. Whether at a six-day cycle race or at a political mass rally, people could really let their hair down here. In fact, it was a place where the atmosphere, according to Goebbels back in 1930, was like 'a madhouse'.[3]

Whereas between 1930 and 1932 the NSDAP held over sixty mass events at the Sports Palace and over forty in both 1933 and 1934, during the following years Goebbels reduced the programme to a few highlights. The Sports Palace became above all the stage for his own performances. Whenever Hitler made a speech there in the years up to 1939—something that happened fairly rarely—it was Goebbels who each time welcomed him like a guest of honour, usually making an introductory speech of his own. Jealously guarding his own position, Goebbels took care that apart from Göring, who by virtue of his exceptional political position enjoyed special privileges, other prominent Nazi leaders appeared before the public here as little as possible, and if they did then it was mostly alongside Goebbels. In this way he ensured that the Sports Palace was chiefly associated with him personally and acquired the status of a sort of ritual site of the 'battle for Berlin' that he, Goebbels, had led during the last years of the Weimar Republic.

After war broke out, Hitler appeared here regularly twice a year, for the 30 January celebration and in the autumn for the opening of the Winter Aid programme. As mentioned above, he was usually introduced by Goebbels. In addition, Hitler made isolated speeches to officer cadets and young officers here, with a few mass rallies on special occasions.

Putting together an audience of people willing to support these events became in time a routine for Goebbels. When on 26 September 1938, at the height of the Sudeten crisis, Hitler made his eagerly awaited speech here, Goebbels had, to use his own words, 'prepared the event down to the last detail. The audience is to consist only of members of the public.'[4] When Hitler charged him in mid-August 1941 with making preparations for a 'proper people's gathering without VIPs', Goebbels performed his task conscientiously: 'I will indeed ensure that he has the right audience.'[5]

In preparation for the rally on 18 February 1943 the front of the massive lectern in the hall had been draped with a swastika flag and two further large swastika flags were hanging from the wall in the background. Apart from these, the enormous space, as befitted the topic, was sparsely decorated, so that the audience's attention would be focused on the banner behind the speaker bearing the slogan 'Total war—Shortest war'.

Numerous prominent people were present at the event, some of whom can be spotted on the existing newsreels. They included the famous actors Heinrich George, Eugen Klöpfer, and Bernhard Minetti. Leading political figures included Albert Speer, the armaments minister, Robert Ley, head of the German Labour Front (DAF), and Fritz Sauckel, Hitler's Plenipotentiary for Labour Deployment. Their presence was assured because Goebbels was to address all three directly in his speech. In addition, we can assume that people named in Goebbels's diary as guests at a party afterwards were also in attendance: Minister of Justice Otto Georg Thierack, as well as the state secretaries* Wilhelm Stuckart, Erhard Milch, and Hellmut Körner.

The speech consists of three parts: first, a general introduction, in which Goebbels confronts his audience with the gravity of the situation, assuring them that he is telling them the truth, and finally concluding from this that they need to act. Second, in the main part of the speech he begins by advancing three propositions which he goes on to justify in detail. Then in the third part the ten questions, which the audience responds to with wild approval, provide the climax and conclusion of the speech.

In terms of content, Goebbels's core argument is that the fight against the mortal threat posed by bolshevism (which he depicts vividly) will demand much greater sacrifices than have hitherto been required, in other words 'total war'. The nation as represented by the audience in the hall is, he claims, not only prepared to accept these sacrifices but in fact demands them. Thus the speech represents a kind of plebiscite for 'total war'.

In addition, there are four secondary strands of argument running through the speech: (1) Behind bolshevism stands Jewry and only the annihilation of Jewry can end the threat from the bolshevist system. (2) The threat is aimed not only at Germany but at the whole of civilized

* Translators' note: State secretaries were the most senior civil servants in a ministry.

Europe, and consequently Europe must be required to make greater efforts to win the war. (3) The ability of the National Socialist government to resist the onslaught from the east is rooted in the experiences gained in the fight with communism during the 'time of struggle'. (4) The measures to implement 'total war' require sacrifices on the part of the whole population, but in particular the upper classes, whose alleged unwillingness to take part in the war effort Goebbels repeatedly criticizes in the course of the speech.

The nature of the event as a kind of 'plebiscite' is of course most evident in the storm of approval at the end of the speech. But in the final analysis the entire speech is constructed as a dialogue with the audience; the vehement support expressed at the end for the ten questions is thus built up from the start in the audience in the hall. Had Goebbels not succeeded in creating this climax in dialogue with the audience, the effect of his ten questions would probably have largely fizzled out. The build-up in support, precisely calibrated and prepared beforehand, is consequently central to the event. Thus it is evident that chants of 'German men, to arms! German women, to work!' did not arise spontaneously in the hall but rather were rehearsed. In addition, we can assume that the NSDAP's Berlin Gau could draw on relevant experience in how to create the desired mood in enclosed spaces. 'They responded to the slightest nuance and applauded in exactly the right places', according to Albert Speer's recollection of a comment that Goebbels allegedly made to him immediately after the speech. Goebbels went on to say that this was 'politically the best trained audience you can find in Germany'.[6] Goebbels knew what he was talking about.

In fact, the sound recording of the speech reveals that almost every time Goebbels raises his voice in order to give particular emphasis to a statement the audience reacts 'spontaneously' through vigorous applause and shouts of acclamation. It responds to the speaker's sarcastic jokes equally 'spontaneously' with laughter or even whoops of support. As a result, anyone interpreting the event must not only analyse Goebbels's rhetoric but pay heed also to the interaction of speaker and audience, as one would in the case of a 'total work of art'.

Let us now take a closer look at the first part of the speech.

National comrades! Party comrades!

[1] *I last spoke to you and the German nation on this very spot barely three weeks ago, when I read out the Führer's proclamation marking the tenth anniversary of the seizure of power. At that point the crisis we face on the eastern front was at its height. On 30 January this year we gathered together, conscious of the heavy blow the nation had suffered in the battle on the Volga, to demonstrate not only our unity and solidarity but also our determination to tackle the immense difficulties confronting us in the fourth year of the war.*

It was deeply moving for me and most likely for you too to discover a few days later that the last heroic soldiers fighting at Stalingrad had been with us at our inspiring rally at the Sports Palace via a radio link. In their final report they radioed that they had heard the Führer's proclamation and, perhaps for the last time, they had joined us with arms raised in singing the national anthem. What exemplary fortitude we see in German fighting men in these momentous times! But what an obligation, particularly for our German homeland, is laid on us all by this fortitude! Stalingrad was and is fate's great wake-up call to the German nation. A nation that can survive such a misfortune, overcome it, and even draw new strength from it is invincible. In my words to you and to the German nation today I'm conscious of the deep sense of obligation I feel and we all feel to the memory of the heroes of Stalingrad.

[2] *I don't know how many millions of people at the front and at home are joining in this rally by radio, but I should like to address you all from the depths of my heart to the depths of yours. I believe the whole German nation is passionately committed to what I have to say tonight. I shall therefore speak with all the respectful seriousness, frankness, and candour that this moment demands. This German nation, raised, trained, and disciplined in National Socialism, can bear the whole truth.* [Shouts of 'Bravo', applause] *It knows the gravity of the Reich's present position and its leaders can therefore call upon it to accept the difficult, indeed extremely difficult, measures arising from the demands of the situation.* [Applause]

We Germans are inured to weakness and debility. The setbacks and misfortunes of war only give us more strength, firm resolve, and the vigour, both mentally and in combat, to overcome all difficulties and obstacles with revolutionary élan.

[3] *Now is not the time to ask how this situation came about. There will be a reckoning, but later, and it will show the German nation and the world the deep and fateful significance of the misfortune that has befallen us during the past weeks. The great and heroic sacrifice made by our soldiers at Stalingrad has been of decisive historical importance for the whole eastern front. It was not in vain and the future will prove it!*

[1] Goebbels begins by reminding his audience of the 'Führer's proclamation' he read out on 30 January. In his introduction to it he had already demanded 'total war', although this catchphrase does not appear in the text of Hitler's own speech. He then refers to defeat at Stalingrad, officially announced only a few days later (on 4 February). He uses a wireless message from the commanders of the 6th Army that had been highlighted in the press to link these two events, reminding his hearers once again of its central passage: the encircled troops had attested that during the broadcast of the proclamation they had, 'while singing the national anthems, joined together, perhaps for the last time, in raising their arms in the German greeting'. This emotional quotation offers Goebbels an opportunity to divert attention from the very real calamity of Stalingrad and to elevate this defeat to mythic status: Stalingrad as 'fate's great wake-up call to the German nation' committed it to a great national effort and was thus a 'misfortune' that could not only be 'survived' but even 'overcome'.

[2] Adopting a solemn and emotionally charged tone, Goebbels now announces that in view of this situation he will speak with 'respectful seriousness, frankness, and candour'. He goes on to say that the nation can cope with the 'whole truth' and is prepared to accept the 'extremely difficult measures arising' from the situation. We then hear the first applause. By emphasizing the seriousness of the situation, the courage to face the truth, and the 'firm resolve' of the nation Goebbels at first adopts an apparently cool and factual tone. After a few minutes, however, he repeatedly introduces heroic notes ('fierce and determined will'; 'revolutionary élan').

[3] Now is not the time, Goebbels continues, to dwell on the causes of defeat. This will be left to a later 'reckoning'. Rather than engaging in fruitless debates they must look forward and act. It is in this context that Goebbels first talks about the crises suffered by the NSDAP in the 'time of struggle', claiming that the

*If I now turn my attention from the recent past to the future, I do so delib-
erately. The matter is urgent. This is no time for sterile debate. We have to act
and act without delay, swiftly and effectively, as has always* [shouts of 'Heil',
applause] *been the way with National Socialism.*

*From the beginning, and in the many crises it has had to withstand and
overcome, the National Socialist movement has responded in this way. And
when it's been under threat, the National Socialist state too has met that threat
with determination and strength of purpose. We aren't ostriches, burying our
heads in the sand so that we can't see the danger. We're courageous enough to
look it straight in the eye, form a cool-headed and ruthless assessment, and then
confront it with determination and heads held high.* [Shouts of 'Heil',
applause] *That is how, as a movement and as a nation, we developed our
supreme virtues, namely a fierce and determined will to destroy and eliminate
any threat, strength of character to overcome all obstacles, a dogged toughness in
pursuing a goal once we have set our minds on it, and a heart of iron that can
resist all assaults from within or without.* [Shouts of 'Bravo', applause]

*That is how it will be today. My task is to give you an unvarnished picture
of the situation and then make clear to you the serious measures that the German
leadership, but also the German nation, must adopt as a consequence.*

*[4] At the moment we are experiencing severe military pressure in the east
and this pressure has temporarily increased so that it resembles that of last winter, in extent if not in kind. I will leave aside the causes for the time being. Today
we must simply accept its existence and consider and adopt the ways and means
at our disposal to relieve it. There is therefore no point in disputing this pressure.
I'm not prepared to give you a misleading impression of the situation, for that
might only lead to your drawing the wrong conclusions and could well lull the
German nation into a false sense of security about its way of life and actions
that would not accord at all with the present situation.*

*The Steppe's onslaught on our venerable continent erupted this winter with
a fury that surpassed any human or historical imagining. The German
Wehrmacht with its allies offers the only viable bulwark against it. In his proclamation of 30 January the Führer raised the serious and pressing question of
what would have become of Germany and Europe if on 30 January 1933 a
bourgeois or democratic regime had come to power instead of the National
Socialist movement. What perils would suddenly have threatened the Reich,
sooner than we could then have suspected? What forces would we have had with
which to defend ourselves? Ten years of National Socialism have sufficed to
make the German nation thoroughly aware of the seriousness of the fateful
problems arising from eastern bolshevism. Now it will be clear why our*

endurance demonstrated before 1933 has in the meantime been imparted through National Socialism to the whole nation, now characterized by a 'determined will', 'strength of character', 'dogged toughness', and 'a heart of iron'. This section too is interrupted by enthusiastic applause.

[4] Now Goebbels comments at length on the 'severe pressure' the military is under and the Steppe's unprecedented 'onslaught on our venerable continent'. Disregarding the causes of the crisis, instead he conjures up the anti-bolshevist tradition and experience of the NSDAP. He justifies the invasion of the Soviet Union in June 1941 as a preventative war 'two minutes to midnight', only to confess candidly immediately after that 'we didn't accurately assess the Soviet Union's war potential'. Now not only the Reich but the whole of the 'west' finds itself facing a dreadful threat and averting it represents an 'enormous task'.

Nuremberg Party rallies so often took place under the banner of the fight against bolshevism. Our aim was to warn the German nation and the world and galvanize the west out of its extraordinary paralysis of mind and will. We wanted to open people's eyes to the appalling historic threats arising from eastern bolshevism, which had led to almost 200 million people being in thrall to Jewish terrorism and was preparing them for a war of aggression against Europe.

When on 22 June 1941 the Führer gave the signal for the German Wehrmacht in the east to attack, we National Socialists knew that this was the start of the decisive battle in this gigantic world struggle. We knew the dangers and difficulties it would cause us. But we also knew that, if we delayed, these dangers and difficulties could only grow and never reduce.

It was two minutes to midnight! Any further delay was liable to destroy the Reich and lead to the complete bolshevization of the European continent.

You will understand why we didn't accurately assess the Soviet Union's war potential because we were misled by the bolshevist regime's elaborate tactics of bluff and disguise. It's only now that we can see its extent and ferocity. The struggle our soldiers in the east are faced with is correspondingly difficult and dangerous beyond all human imagining. It demands the whole of the nation's strength. The Reich and the continent of Europe are under threat in a way that puts all previous threats to the west in the shade. If we were to fail in this, we would have squandered the chance to fulfil our historic mission. Everything we've built up and achieved thus far pales in the face of the enormous task directly confronting the German Wehrmacht and indirectly the German nation.

[5] First I shall address a world audience and present it with three propositions regarding our fight against the bolshevist threat in the east.

The first proposition is: If the German Wehrmacht were not capable of destroying the threat from the east, the Reich and shortly thereafter the whole of Europe would capitulate to bolshevism. [Weak applause]

The second of these three propositions is: The German Wehrmacht and the German nation along with their allies are the only ones who have the power to rescue Europe completely from this threat.

The third proposition is: The danger is imminent! Swift and radical action must be taken, otherwise it will be too late! [Loud applause]

[6] On the first proposition I want to make these detailed comments. Bolshevism has always openly avowed that it aims to bring about revolution, not only in Europe but throughout the world, and to plunge the latter into

[5] This statement of the problem leads into the main section of the speech, which Goebbels begins by reading out his three core propositions. He claims they are addressed to a 'world audience' and he will repeatedly introduce a European dimension into the remarks that follow.

The three propositions are as follows: (1) The German Reich and Europe will be overrun by bolshevism if the Wehrmacht proves unable to stem the onslaught from the east. (2) Only the Wehrmacht and the German nation with its allies possess the power to save Europe from bolshevism. (3) In view of the threat there must be rapid and effective action. The hesitant reaction to the first two propositions is striking, whereas the third is enthusiastically applauded.

[6] Goebbels's exposition of the first proposition lasts barely ten minutes, and he immediately expands its scope. First of all, he emphasizes in particular that the openly proclaimed aim of

bolshevist chaos. From the inception of the bolshevist Soviet Union this has been the aim that the Kremlin has stood for ideologically and has pursued in practice. It's obvious that the closer Stalin and the other Soviet leaders believe they are to realizing their destructive aims, the more they try to disguise and obscure them. We National Socialists aren't deceived by this. We're not timid types who stare like hypnotized rabbits at a snake until it gobbles them up. We aim to recognize the danger in good time and confront it in an effective and timely fashion. We can see through not only the ideology of bolshevism but also its tactics, for we have already done battle with them, and with outstanding success, in the realm of domestic politics. The Kremlin cannot deceive us. In a fourteen-year struggle before we took power and in a ten-year one after taking power, we exposed its intentions and dastardly plots to hoodwink the world.

The aim of bolshevism is world revolution brought about by the Jews. They want to create chaos in the Reich and in Europe so that they can use the nations' resulting sense of hopelessness and despair to set up their international capitalist tyranny, disguised as bolshevism. [Loud cries of indignation]

[7] *I don't need to expand on what that would mean for the German nation. The bolshevization of the Reich would lead to the liquidation of our entire intelligentsia and leadership and our working masses being taken into bolshevist–Jewish slavery. That is their aim. As the Führer said in his proclamation on 30 January, in Moscow they're looking for battalions of slave labourers for the Siberian tundra. Our battle fronts are facing the revolt of the Steppe and the invasion from the east that surges against our front lines with daily increasing force is nothing more or less than the attempt to repeat the historic ravages that imperilled our continent so often in the past.*

This is an immediate and acute threat not only for us but for all European powers. Don't think that bolshevism, if victorious, would be stopped at our borders by a paper agreement. It's pursuing a policy of aggression and of waging aggressive war with the aim of bolshevizing all countries and nations.

When set against these indisputable intentions, paper declarations from the Kremlin or guarantees issued by London or Washington don't impress us! We know that in the east we're dealing with political devilry that doesn't abide by the normal rules governing relations between people and states. When for example England's Lord Beaverbrook declares that the leadership of Europe must be handed over to the bolshevists [cries of indignation]*, or when Brown, a leading American–Jewish journalist, expands on this in a cynical communiqué suggesting that a bolshevization of Europe might actually represent a solution to our continent's problems, we can be sure what these Jews have in mind.* [Shouts] bolshevism has always been world revolution. Since the early 1920s the danger posed by this enemy has been well known and so it is also known that bolshevism's real aim is 'world revolution brought about by the Jews'. The latter intend, he claims, to set up an 'international capitalist tyranny, disguised as bolshevism'.

[7] In a crude inversion of the policy of annihilation as practised by the National Socialist occupiers in the east, Goebbels claims that for the Reich this means the 'liquidation of our entire intelligentsia and leadership and our working masses being taken into bolshevist–Jewish slavery'. Bolshevism will, however, also extend its dominion over other European countries, not least with support from Jews in those countries. This passage in particular, in which Goebbels elaborates on this threat, quoting alleged western supporters of these conspiracies, fantasizing about 'Jewish liquidation squads', and conjuring up the prospect of the destruction of 'civilizations thousands of years old', is interrupted repeatedly by agitated interjections and chanting from the audience.

The European powers are facing an existential question. The west is in danger! [Shouts] *Whether or not their governments and intelligentsias recognize it is completely beside the point.*

As far as the German nation and its leaders are concerned at least, we are not prepared to give in to this threat in the slightest degree. [Loud cries, applause, excited shouting] *Behind the advancing Soviet divisions we can already see Jewish liquidation squads and behind these terror looms—the spectre of starving millions and complete anarchy in Europe. Again, we see international Jewry revealed as the devilish catalyst to decomposition. It gains a positively cynical satisfaction from plunging the world into deepest chaos and destroying civilizations thousands of years old that it never cared about. We know, therefore, what a historic task we face. Two thousand years of western civilization are under threat. It's a threat that cannot be exaggerated but it is also typical that, if one speaks the truth about it, international Jewry across the world protests vigorously. We have reached the point in Europe where it's impossible to call a threat a threat if it's caused by the Jews! That doesn't prevent us National Socialists from speaking the truth, however. We have never feared the Jews, and we fear them today less than ever!* [Cries of 'Heil', vigorous and sustained applause]

We spoke out earlier in our domestic struggles when communist Jewry was exploiting democratic Jewry in the Berliner Tageblatt *and the* Vossische Zeitung *to minimize and trivialize a threat that was becoming more ominous by the day; they lulled those endangered sections of our nation into a false sense of security and deadened their powers of resistance. If we didn't eliminate this threat we would already glimpse the spectre of hunger, misery, and forced labour for millions looming for the German nation; we would see this most venerable continent shaken to its foundations, beneath its ruins the historic heritage of western humanity. That's the challenge we're facing.*

[8] *My second proposition is this: Only the German Reich with its allies is capable of averting this danger. The European states including England claim to be strong enough to oppose any bolshevization of the European continent promptly and effectively, if the situation should arise.* [Laughter] *Such a claim is childish and not worth refuting, for if the strongest military power in the world—the German Reich—were unable to crush the threat of bolshevism, who would then be up to it?* [Cries of 'No one!' Applause]

The neutral European states perhaps? [Cries of 'No!'] *They possess neither the potential nor the military means nor anything like the mental preconditions* [cries of agreement, sustained applause] *to offer bolshevism even the slightest resistance. If the situation arose, they would simply be flattened in a few days by its mobile robot divisions. In the capitals of the medium-sized and*

[8] The elucidation of the second proposition, namely that only the German Reich and its allies can avert this danger, follows on almost seamlessly from these comments. Goebbels works himself up more and more into an anti-Jewish diatribe. Its central theme echoes one of the leitmotivs of German propaganda since mid-1941, namely that the alliance between the Soviet Union and the Anglo-Saxon powers with their fundamentally opposing political systems was being held together in essence by an international Jewish world conspiracy (which in the east presents as bolshevism and in the west as 'plutocratic capitalism'). Thus National Socialist Germany has the legitimate right, indeed is positively compelled if it wants to preserve itself, to 'wage war against the Jews' both at home and abroad.

smaller European states people take comfort in the notion that the bolshevist threat must be resisted mentally. [Laughter] *That brings back desperate memories of the bourgeois parties of the centre in 1932 declaring that communism could only be defeated with the weapons of the mind.* [Interjection, murmuring] *Even then, such a claim seemed to us simply too daft to be taken seriously. Eastern bolshevism isn't only terrorist in doctrine but terrorist in practice. It pursues its aims with infernal thoroughness, drawing on all its internal resources without any regard for the happiness, prosperity, or peace of the peoples under its yoke.*

What would England and America do if the worst came to the worst and the European continent fell into the arms of bolshevism? Does London perhaps intend to persuade Europe that bolshevism would stop at the English Channel because that was the agreement? I have already referred to the fact that bolshevism has its foreign legions already in place on the soil of all democratic states in the form of their communist parties. None of these states can claim to be immune to an internal process of bolshevization. In a recent by-election to the English House of Commons the independent (in other words communist) candidate in a constituency that up to then had been a very safe Conservative seat gained 10,000 votes out of a total of 22,000. That means that in a very short time in this constituency alone the parties of the right have lost around 10,000 votes, half of the total votes, to the communists. This is just one more proof that the bolshevist threat exists even in England and that simply ignoring it will not make it go away. In our view, any territorial undertakings the Soviet Union enters into are worthless. Bolshevism regularly uses ideology and not only military strength to draw its borders and therein lies the threat it poses of disregarding national boundaries. In other words, the world does not have a choice between a Europe returning to its old state of fragmentation and a Europe being reordered under the Axis powers. It has the choice only between a Europe under the military protection of the Axis and a bolshevist Europe. [Applause]

Furthermore, I am convinced that, in spite of the lamentations of the lords and archbishops in London, in practice they have no intention of opposing the bolshevist threat to the European states in the event of a further advance by the Soviet armies. Jewry has penetrated the intellectual and political life of the Anglo–Saxon states so deeply that they are unwilling to recognize and acknowledge this threat. Just as in the Soviet Union it disguises itself as bolshevism, in the Anglo-Saxon states it masquerades as plutocratic capitalism. The Jewish race is famous for their powers of mimicry, systematically adapting to their environment. Their method has always been to put their host countries to sleep and paralyse their powers of resistance to the acute and life-threatening danger they pose. [Shouts]

Understanding these issues early on made us recognize that, contrary to appearances, the duality of international plutocracy and international bolshevism is by no means nonsensical but rather represents a profound causal relationship. Above and beyond our own country, faux-civilized Western European Jewry and the Jewry of the eastern ghettos are working in concert, putting Europe in mortal danger, even though the English will not admit it.

I do not flatter myself that what I say can arouse public opinion in neutral states, let alone in hostile ones. Nor is that my aim or intention. I know that tomorrow the English press will be up in arms about me, screaming that because of our problems on the eastern front I was putting out the first feelers towards a peace. [Laughter] *That is out of the question. In Germany today no one has any thoughts of a grubby compromise. The whole nation has thoughts only of a tough war!* [Loud and sustained applause, shouting]

But as the responsible spokesman for the leading country on this continent I claim for myself the sovereign right to call a threat a threat, if it endangers not only our own country but our entire continent. We National Socialists have always seen it as our duty to sound the alarm against international Jewry's attempts to plunge the continent of Europe into chaos, after it created in bolshevism a terrorist military power that poses an immeasurable threat.

[9] *The third proposition I wish to expand on is that the danger is imminent. The signs of intellectual paralysis evident in the western European democracies in the face of their most deadly threat are truly terrifying and international Jewry is reinforcing them as much as it can. In our own struggle for power in our own country Jewish newspapers had anaesthetized resistance to communism and it was only revived by the National Socialist movement. This is precisely what is now happening in other nations. Yet again Jewry is shown to be the incarnation of evil, the demon of decay personified and the carrier of chaos, destroying civilization on an international level.*

And, just in passing, this explains our rigorous policies towards the Jews, even though the Berlin Jews are now mobilizing their usual bleeding hearts brigade. [Calls of 'String them up!']

[10] *Jewry represents in our view a direct threat to all countries.* [Cries of 'String them up', applause] *We don't care how other nations defend themselves against this threat. How we defend ourselves, on the other hand, is our*

[9] Goebbels's elaboration of the third proposition, namely that the threat is imminent, is similarly deeply anti-Semitic. He characterizes Jews among other things as the 'incarnation of evil', 'the demon of decay personified' and the origin of a chaos that is destroying international civilization. Almost in passing he suggests that this background 'explains our rigorous policies towards the Jews, even though the Berlin Jews are now mobilizing their usual bleeding hearts brigade'. The latter comment alludes to the fact that the Jewish population not yet deported from Berlin to the east consisted mainly of older Jews, who had been deprived of their property and sources of income and forced to wear the yellow star. Their wretched appearance elicited small gestures of sympathy and support from sections of the Berlin population. Before the end of the month, it should be noted, a large-scale campaign (Aktion) to arrest and deport the Berlin Jews still working in the armaments industry was to follow.

[10] While Goebbels is speaking on this topic, calls of 'String them up' can be heard in the hall. This response was part of a ritual that can be traced back to the beginnings of the Nazi

own business and we will not tolerate any objections to it. [Loud applause, excited shouting]

Jewry infects—Jewry is an infectious disease. If our enemies abroad protest hypocritically against our anti-Jewish policies and shed crocodile tears over our anti-Jewish measures, that won't stop us from doing what it is necessary. Germany, at any rate, has no intention of yielding to this Jewish menace but will rather resist it promptly, if necessary by the complete root-and-branch extermin—... exclusion of Jewry. [Loud applause, cries of excitement, laughter]

All these considerations are at the heart of the Reich's military difficulties in the east. The war of mechanized robots against Germany and Europe has reached its peak. The German nation along with its Axis partners is fulfilling a European mission in the truest sense of the word by warding off this direct and serious threat to its existence by force of arms. We shan't be deterred by the universal outcry of international Jewry from the courageous and honourable prosecution of this gigantic struggle against a world-wide pestilence. It can and must end only in victory! [Cries of 'Heil', sustained and loud applause, shouts, chants of 'German men, to arms!', 'German women, to work!']

movement but also occurs in the demonstrations of other radical anti-Semitic groups. Fanatical group members responded repeatedly to a speaker's anti-Jewish attacks with similar death threats, thus continuing his train of thought and relieving him of having to give details of what he planned to do with the Jews. This 'meeting of minds' between audience and speaker is also evident on 18 February 1943 in the Sports Palace. How Germany is going to defend itself against the threat posed by the Jews is, as Goebbels continues, 'our own business and we will not tolerate any objections to it'. The audience responds with loud applause and excited shouting. He then explicitly tackles 'protest' and 'crocodile tears', with which 'enemies abroad' react to Germany's 'anti-Jewish policies'. Referring to the 'complete root-and-branch exclusion of Jewry' he adds a 'slip of the tongue' by half-saying 'extermination' (Ausrottung) instead of 'exclusion' (Ausschaltung). Far from denying the information current both in Allied propaganda and in the rumour mills in Germany about the systematic murder of the Jews, he takes the opportunity expressly to confirm it.[7] The audience picks up on the hint and responds with loud applause, shouts, and laughter. Two minutes later he again causes a storm of applause by bellowing that Germany will not be deterred 'by the universal outcry of international Jewry' from 'this gigantic struggle against a world-wide pestilence'.

These statements by Goebbels repeat the line already taken for a considerable time by Hitler and other leading Nazi political figures, namely that of using carefully targeted hints to confirm in general terms the rumours circulating about the murder of the European Jews, though without betraying details of the full-scale programme of murder. Most recently Hitler had declared in his proclamation of 30 January that 'this pathogen' had to be 'got rid of', and on the same occasion Göring had warned in a radio address that if the Germans were defeated 'the Jew' would 'take revenge on us' and annihilate the German nation.[8]

Whereas many Germans evidently shrank from drawing from these statements and from other information from various sources about the persecution of the Jews the obvious and shocking conclusion that their own government was actually in the process of committing the crime of the century, the National Socialist activists who made up a large part of the audience in the

[11] *The battle for Stalingrad came to symbolize this resistance to the revolt of the Steppe. It had thus acquired not only military but also profound intellectual and psychological significance for the German nation. It was there that our eyes were fully opened to the issues arising from this war. We want no more false hopes and illusions. We want to face the facts fearlessly, however hard and cruel they may be. For the history of our Party and our state has shown every time that a threat acknowledged is soon a threat abolished. Our future bitterest defensive battles in the east will exemplify this heroic resistance. They will place demands on our soldiers and their weapons to an extent unfamiliar to us from any previous campaigns. In the east a pitiless war is raging. The Führer was right to say in his proclamation on the 30 January that at the end of it there wouldn't be victors and vanquished but only survivors and annihilated.*

The German nation has clearly understood this. Its sound instincts have found their own way through the confused tangle of intellectual and psychological difficulties of this war and its daily contingencies. Today we are fully aware that the kind of Blitzkrieg used in Poland and in the campaign in the west has only limited relevance to the east. Here the German nation is fighting for its very survival. During this battle we have come to realize that the German nation must defend its most sacred possessions, its families, its women and children, its beautiful, pristine countryside, its towns and villages, its cultural heritage stretching back two thousand years, and everything that for us makes life worth living.

Of course, bolshevism has not the slightest understanding of the richness of our national heritage and if necessary would disregard it completely. It does not accord even its own people that privilege. For twenty-five years the Soviet Union has been maximizing its bolshevist war potential to an extent we could not imagine and which we as a result miscalculated. This terrorist Jewry has utilized 200 million people in Russia, combining its own cynical methods and practices with the stolid toughness of the Russian race and as a result posing an even greater threat to the civilized European nations. In the east a whole nation is being forced to fight. Men, women, and, yes, even children are being forced not only to work in the munitions factories but to fight in the war itself.

Sports Palace were unlikely to have had such scruples. Significantly, in October 1942 the Party apparatus had received a special circular from the head of the Party Chancellery, Martin Bormann, informing them about the background to the rumours about the Jews in such a way as to imply confirmation of them.[9] The positively enthusiastic reactions of the audience to Goebbels's anti-Semitic tirades demonstrate clearly that speaker and audience were in agreement about anti-Jewish policies that were radical and cruel to an unprecedented degree.

[11] After some fifteen minutes of anti-Semitic polemic Goebbels returns to the topic of Stalingrad and the war in the east in general. At its end, he says, referring to a remark of Hitler's, there will only be 'survivors and annihilated'. Everything was at stake: the lives of women and children, the pristine beauty of the German countryside, the continued existence of towns and villages, the fruits of two thousand years of civilization. This was all being put at risk by the ruthless actions of a gigantic war machine that was able to draw on 200 million people. 'Terrorist Jewry' had combined with the 'stolid toughness of the Russian race'.

[12] *Two hundred million crude and dull-witted people are confronting us there, some in terror of the GPU‡ and some trapped in a diabolical ideology. The tanks massed this winter on our eastern front are the upshot of twenty-five years of social misery and misfortune suffered by the bolshevist nation. If we aren't resigned to throwing in the towel we must respond with appropriate countermeasures.*

This is my firm belief: in the long run we can only crush the bolshevist threat by using if not the same methods then equally effective ones! [Shouts of 'Bravo' and applause] *The German people are facing the most serious issue in this war, namely how to generate the determination to commit everything they can in order to preserve everything they have and to secure everything they need for the future.* [Applause]

It's no longer about maintaining a high standard of living today at the expense of our ability to defend ourselves against the east. The point is rather that we must boost our defensive capabilities at the expense of a high standard of living that is no longer right for the times. [Shouts of support, applause] *This has nothing whatever to do with copying bolshevist methods. In the past in our struggle with the Communist Party we adopted different methods from those we used against the bourgeois parties. We were up against an opponent we had to defeat with different methods for it used terror in order to crush the National Socialist movement. But terror is not broken by intellectual arguments but must be answered with terror!* [Shouts of 'Heil', loud applause]

The intellectual threat posed by bolshevism is well known and undisputed, even abroad. In addition to the intellectual threat, however, it now represents for us and for Europe a direct military danger. Countering it only with intellectual arguments would probably produce unbridled hilarity in the Kremlin. We are neither so stupid nor so purblind as to attempt to fight bolshevism with such inadequate means. Nor do we wish to exemplify the proverb that only the most stupid calves choose their own butchers. We are determined to defend our lives with every means possible, regardless of whether the wider world recognizes the need for this struggle or not! [Shouts of approval, applause]

Total war is therefore what this moment demands. [Shouts of 'Heil', applause]

There must be an end to bourgeois squeamishness that even in this fateful struggle wishes to operate on the principle: [crescendo of shouting, applause that carries on past the next sentence] *Make me an omelette but don't break any eggs.‡ The danger we are facing is enormous and so the efforts we*

† Since 1922 GPU (or OGPU) had been the abbreviation for the Soviet Union's secret police.
‡ Translators' note: Literally 'Wash me, but don't get me wet.'

[12] With an urgent call to adopt suitable 'countermeasures', Goebbels moves on to the point where he demands concrete and radical steps to ramp up the war effort. He begins with a series of challenges to which the audience responds with increasing passion, interrupting him again and again after a few sentences with noisy applause. Now, almost halfway through his speech, Goebbels for the first time utters the event's key slogan, which all in the hall have been waiting for: 'Total war is therefore what this moment demands.'

make to oppose it must also be enormous. So the moment has come to take off the kid gloves. [Shouting, calls of 'Heil', applause] *Now we must use our fists!* [Shouts of 'Yes!', brief applause]

[13] *We can't go on making only patchy and superficial use of the resources not only of our own country but of those significant parts of Europe at our disposal. We must exploit them fully and as quickly and thoroughly as possible, both organizationally and practically. A false sense of concern would be utterly misplaced. Europe's future depends on our struggle in the east. We are ready to protect it. The German nation is offering its most precious blood for this struggle. The rest of Europe should at least be prepared to offer its labour!* [Shouts of 'Heil', loud applause] *Those in the rest of Europe who don't understand this struggle today will tomorrow fall to their knees and thank us for taking it upon ourselves.* [Cries of 'Hear, hear', applause]

We're not even irritated when our enemies abroad claim that the measures we're now taking to totalize the war are similar to those used in bolshevism. [Murmurs] *They declare hypocritically that in these circumstances the fight against bolshevism must therefore be superfluous because* we *are bolshevists.* [Indignant shouts, interjection of 'But without Jews', laughter]

What is important here is not the method of destroying bolshevism but the aim, the removal of the threat! [Shouts of 'Bravo', applause] *The question is not, therefore, whether the methods we use are pleasant or unpleasant but only if they are successful. As National Socialist leaders we at any rate are now determined to stop at nothing. We shall take action regardless of who objects!* [Shouts of 'Hear, hear', 'Bravo', applause]

[13] Before going into greater detail about the burdens that will be placed on the German population by total war, Goebbels first spells out what he demands of the 'significant parts of Europe at our disposal', by which he means those parts under German occupation, as well, presumably, as those smaller 'allies' dependent on Germany. Their war potential must be utilized completely; and as Germany is defending this Europe with its own blood it is fully entitled to demand that Europe should 'at least be prepared to offer its labour'.

This passage makes clear why Goebbels repeatedly emphasizes the European dimension of the 'Jewish–bolshevist' challenge: He wants his audience to know that they are not the only ones who will have to shoulder a considerably increased burden of work, but that this will also be the lot above all of the inhabitants of German-dominated Europe. At the start of 1943 the Greater German Reich contained a total of about 5 million foreign 'workers'. The vast majority were men and women recruited by force who, especially if they came from Eastern Europe, were subject to merciless exploitation as well as to poor, even wretched, working and living conditions or were prisoners of war, mainly from France, Poland, and the Soviet Union. By saying that Europe must 'at least be prepared to offer its labour', Goebbels was not merely justifying this policy but was supplying a reason to treat foreign slave workers in an even more brutal fashion.

Ultimately the European dimension of the speech is also directed at the wider German public and its sense of self-interest. It is therefore precisely not to be understood as an attempt to mobilize the whole of Europe against the bolshevist threat. There would have been no basis for this in earlier propaganda: In the months leading up to this speech German propaganda had carefully avoided giving any impression of an intention to bolster the German war effort by making political concessions to allied or occupied countries. Proposals from Goebbels's ministry, from the Foreign Ministry, and from other departments to publish something along the lines of a European proclamation giving the countries in question at least some kind of prospect, however

[14] *We refuse* ... [sustained applause] *we refuse any longer to weaken Germany's war capabilities in the interests of maintaining a high, at times almost peacetime, standard of living for a particular social stratum, thus putting our war effort at risk.* [Shout of 'Bastards!'] *On the contrary, we shall voluntarily accept a significant reduction in this standard of living in order to boost our war potential as quickly and effectively as possible.* [Shouts of 'Bravo', enthusiastic applause]

What's more, as I hear from endless numbers of letters at home and gestures of support from the front, the German nation as a whole is of one mind. Everyone knows that if we were to lose this war we would be annihilated. This nation and its leaders are therefore determined to defend themselves in the most radical manner! The broad mass of working people in our nation don't accuse the government of being too ruthless but, if anything, of not being ruthless enough. [Shouts of 'Bravo', loud applause] *Ask people the length and breadth of the country and the answer is always the same: Today the most radical measures are only just radical enough and the most total ones only just total enough to secure victory.* [Shouts of 'Bravo', loud applause] *Thus total war concerns the whole German nation. No one can have even the remotest justification for trying to evade its demands. When I proclaimed total war on this very spot in my speech of 30 January, I was met with a storm of approval from the* ill-defined, of a future in a German-dominated Europe had all come to nothing as a result of resistance from Hitler. He was unwilling to be pinned down in any way in his plans for post-war Europe, and that included even promises made purely for propagandistic purposes. Although late in 1942 Goebbels had raised this issue in two articles for Das Reich, Hitler did not support any further initiatives.[10]

The National Socialist regime could not therefore count on a wave of European solidarity that extended beyond the narrow confines of fellow fascists in the allied or occupied countries. In addition, in the occupied Soviet territories it had not only committed unprecedented crimes but had burnt its boats as far as gaining some support for German war policy was concerned by failing to offer concessions to the native population (for example, by granting religious freedom or ending the system of collective farms).[11] Hitler and Alfred Rosenberg, the Minister for the East, forced Goebbels to shelve an 'Eastern Proclamation' on which he had been working in late 1942/early 1943, offering the prospect, at least for the future, of such concessions.[12]

[14] After Goebbels has called for additional contributions from the European countries 'at our disposal', he makes it clear that his demands on the German population are aimed first and foremost at a 'particular social stratum', namely at those on the home front who continue to afford themselves 'a high, at times almost peacetime, standard of living'. He knows, he claims, that although the vast majority of the nation is prepared to make any sacrifice necessary, it also expects the state to take measures against 'a small, passive section' attempting 'to shirk' the 'burdens and the responsibilities' of war. 'No account of class or profession' was therefore to be taken. Everyone was to be exhorted, indeed compelled, to fulfil their duty to the nation.

As on 30 January, for these passages suggestive of 'class struggle' Goebbels repeatedly receives the most enthusiastic applause. Voices in the crowd also call for the 'bastards' to be summarily strung up. In the course of this attack on the allegedly still privileged classes Goebbels continues to raise the temperature, not least by attempting to intensify rhetorically his demands for radical and total action by using ever more extreme superlatives ('today the most radical measures are only just radical *assembled mass of people. So I can state with confidence that the leadership's measures are in complete accord with the whole German nation at home and at the front.* [Shout of 'Yes', loud and sustained applause] *The nation is prepared . . .* [Shout, some applause] *the nation is prepared to bear any burden, even the heaviest, and is willing to make any sacrifice that might lead to victory. It must be said . . .* [Shouts of 'Bravo', applause], *it must be said, however, that this assumes that burdens are shared equitably.* [Shouts of 'Bravo', loud applause] *The government mustn't allow the overwhelming majority of the nation to carry the entire burden of the war while a small, passive section of it attempts to shirk its burdens and responsibilities.* [Shout of 'String them up', applause] *The measures we have already taken and must still take will therefore be an expression of the spirit of National Socialist justice. We shall take no account of class or profession!* [Shouts of 'Bravo', loud applause]

Rich and poor, high and lowly, must make the same sacrifices. In this most crucial phase of our fight for survival everyone will be required, and if necessary compelled, to fulfil his or her duty to the nation. [Shouts of 'Bravo', applause] *In so doing we know we're acting in concert with the national will of our people. We would rather do too much than too little to achieve victory. No war in history was ever lost because the leaders had too many soldiers. Many were lost, however, because the opposite was the case.*

I've already stated publicly that the decisive task today for the outcome of the war is to take the most radical measures to present the Führer with an operational reserve that will enable him finally to launch an offensive in the coming spring and summer, as he urgently wishes to do! [Shouts of 'Heil', very loud and sustained applause, shouting] *The more power we put into the Führer's hands, the more devastating this blow will be. So this is not the time to harbour notions of peace. The German nation has every reason to think only of war! This doesn't serve to lengthen it but to speed it up. The most total and radical war is also the shortest.* [Applause] *We must go on the offensive again in the east! We must mobilize the necessary manpower, which is still abundant, not only through organization and bureaucracy but through improvisation.* [Shouts] *Complicated bureaucratic procedures slow things down, while the clock is ticking and urgency is required. In the past too, when the National Socialist movement was fighting the democratic state, we sometimes abandoned cumbersome ways of doing things. Then too we often lived hand-to-mouth and improvised in order to achieve our political goals. That must be our method again today. So it's time to get the stragglers moving!* [Shouts of 'Bravo', loud applause] *They must be shaken out of their complacency!* [Shouts of 'Yes'] *We can't wait for them to come to their senses on their own, when it may be too late.* [Interjection] *The alarm must* enough and the most total ones only just total enough to secure victory'; 'The most total and radical war is also the shortest'). The efforts being demanded of the nation, he declares to his audience, ultimately serve the purpose of supplying the 'Führer' with an 'operational reserve' at home that will finally enable him the following spring and summer to launch a new offensive, 'as he urgently wishes to do'.

Goebbels now moves on to the details of the measures planned, and in some cases already introduced, though not before aiming another sideswipe at 'certain people' who were trying 'somehow or other to avoid these burdens'. They must be subject to 'draconian punishments'. Significantly, Goebbels therefore mentions first a series of measures that are in themselves not of 'vital importance' for the war but seem necessary to 'uphold morale at home and at the front'. Their purpose is to ensure the correct 'optics of the war', to use Goebbels's phrase, an allusion to the title of an article he had published shortly before in *Das Reich*.

sound throughout the nation! Millions of hands must set to work right away up and down the land. [Interjection]

The measures that we've already taken and must still take—I'll explain in more detail in the remainder of my speech—make inroads into the whole of the private sphere and public life. We're aware of that. The sacrifices that individual citizens must make are sometimes serious, but they're insignificant when set against the sacrifices they would have to make if they refused to make them and thus brought the worst disaster down on the nation. It is better to operate at the right moment than to delay until the illness has really taken hold. [Shouts of 'Bravo'] *It is no good staying the surgeon's hand as he makes the incision, let alone accusing him of criminal assault.* [Shout of 'Never!'] *He's cutting not to kill but to save the patient's life!*

Again, I must emphasize that the greater the sacrifices demanded of the German nation the more pressing the need that they should be fairly shared. The nation wants this. No one today bridles at accepting even the heaviest burdens of war. But of course anyone would be annoyed if certain people always try to avoid these burdens. [Murmurs] *The National Socialist government has both the moral and the political duty to counter such attempts decisively, unflinchingly, and if necessary through draconian punishments!* [Shouts of Heil, loud applause] *Leniency would be entirely misplaced in such cases and might gradually lead to people becoming upset and confused and result in a serious threat to public morale at a time of war.*

Hence we're obliged to introduce a series of measures that, while not in themselves of vital importance for the war, nevertheless appear necessary to uphold morale at home and at the front. The optics of the war, in other words the external image of the war, is also of decisive political importance in this fourth year of war.

In view of the superhuman sacrifices made daily, the front has a fundamental right to expect that absolutely no one at home claims the right to live untouched by the war and its obligations. [Murmurs] *Not only the front demands this but also the overwhelming majority of decent citizens at home.* [Shouts of 'Bravo', applause] *Hard workers putting in ten, twelve, and sometimes fourteen hours a day have the right not to see the work-shy sprawled right next to them and even regarding them, the conscientious, as stupid or not crafty enough.* [Shouts of agreement, applause] *The homeland in its entirety must remain pristine and unsullied. Nothing must dull its wartime image.*

[15] *A series of measures has therefore been introduced with this new optical aspect of the war in mind. We have, for example, ordered the closure of bars and nightclubs.* [Enthusiastic approval, applause, shouting] *I can't imagine that*

[15] In concrete terms he announces the closure of bars, night-clubs, and luxury venues and also the shutdown of 'shops and businesses selling luxury goods for outward show', fashion

there are still people today who conscientiously fulfil their war duties and at the same time sit late into the night in pubs and clubs. [Shout of 'That's only for shirkers!'] *I can only conclude that they don't take their war duties particularly seriously. We have closed down these clubs because they were beginning to be a nuisance and blurring the image of the war.* [Interjection] *And the nation won't put up with it. In doing this we aren't in any way wanting to be killjoys. After the war we shall gladly go back to a policy of live and let live.* [Applause] *But during the war our motto is fight and let fight!* [Shouts of 'Bravo', enthusiastic applause]

Luxury restaurants, where the effort and expense are quite out of proportion to the effect achieved, will also be closed. [Shouts of 'Bravo', more interjections, murmurs] *It may be* [Shout of 'There are no workers in there!' Laughter] *that the odd person here and there sees their main task as looking after their stomach, even in wartime.* [Amusement] *Unfortunately we can no longer indulge such people. Our fighting men at the front from privates to Field Marshals eat from field kitchens, so I believe we aren't asking too much if we at home force everyone at least to respect the most fundamental rules of community!* [Shouts of 'Bravo', lively applause] *We can go back to being gourmets after the war.* [Laughter] *Today we have more important things to do than look after our stomachs. Countless shops and businesses selling luxury goods for outward show have also been closed. For general consumers they had often simply become a provocation.* [Interjection] *There was hardly anything there that the average person could buy, or at best only if on odd occasions it was possible to pay in butter or eggs rather than with money.* [Some laughter, applause] *What is the point of shops if they don't sell any goods and only consume electric light, heating, and human labour that we are badly short of elsewhere, above all in armaments production. Don't object that we're impressing foreign countries by maintaining this semblance of peacetime.* [Laughter] *Foreign countries will be impressed above all by victory!* [Enthusiastic applause]

During the time of struggle we were the poor Nazis! Then when we had won everyone wanted to be friends with us! [Shouts of 'Bravo', applause] *Once we're victorious in this war too everyone will want to be our friend.* [Laughter] *If we were defeated we could probably count our friends on the fingers of one hand. We've therefore done away with illusions that obscure the reality of war. We'll give people who stand around idly in empty shops some useful work in the war economy.* [Loud approval, applause] *This process is already in train and will be completed by 15 March. Naturally, it represents an enormous reorganization of our entire economic life. Hundreds of thousands of people will be on the move. We're not proceeding haphazardly, for we're not* houses, and expensive hairdressing salons. Government offices will work 'faster and less bureaucratically' and work will go on until the cases in hand are dealt with or part of the workforce can be released for important war work. There are then some ironic comments about the pointless routine of bureaucracy as well as criticisms of 'frivolous jobs', which go down as well with the audience as his rants against superfluous restaurants and shops. They also respond positively to Goebbels's reference to a ban he has ordered on horse riding in Berlin, and also to his tirades against 'empty-headed riff-raff' in spa resorts and 'unemployed leisure travellers' on the railways. At the same time, the 'working population' must still have 'leisure facilities', and so theatres, cinemas, music venues, and sports facilities would be kept open. As in his speech of 30 January, in striking this note of 'class struggle' Goebbels is harking back to the anti-bourgeois public persona he so assiduously cultivated in particular during the 'time of struggle' in what was then 'red' Berlin. The appeal to a certain social envy of the privileged classes was, however, a theme of Goebbels propaganda that regularly recurred even in the years after 1933.

Almost a third of the two hours of Goebbels's speech is taken up with his remarks on a 'Spartan existence for all' and on renouncing everything that in his own words is not 'of vital importance'.

flustered, nor do we wish to accuse anyone unjustly or dole out criticism and blame indiscriminately.We're simply doing what is necessary, but we're doing it swiftly and effectively.

We would rather wear patched and darned clothes for a few years than go around in rags for a few centuries. [Shouts of 'Bravo,' lively applause] *What, for example, is the point of fashion houses today if they consume light, heat, and human labour?* [Interjections] *After the war, when we've time and inclination again, they will of course come back. Why do we need hairdressing salons, which promote a cult of beauty requiring an enormous amount of time and labour? They're perfectly pleasant in peacetime but in wartime they're superfluous at the very least. Our women and girls should not be worried.* [Laughter] *When our soldiers return home victorious, they'll find them attractive even without their peacetime hairdos and make-up.* [Laughter, applause]

Government offices will in future work faster and less bureaucratically. It doesn't make a good impression if when the bell rings at the end of an eight-hour shift the files are closed and work comes to an end. [Shouts of 'Bravo', applause, interjections] *People are not there for the sake of the offices, rather the offices are there for the people.* [Shouts of 'Bravo', vigorous applause] *Don't work until the bell rings but until the work is done.* [Shouts of 'Bravo'] *That's the rule in wartime. If the Führer can do it, his hired servants can do it too.* [Shouts of 'Bravo', vigorous applause] *If there's not enough work to fill longer work-ing hours 10, 20, or 30 per cent of the staff should be transferred to essential war work* [some applause] *and thus free up a corresponding number of men for the front. That's the problem!* [Sustained and vigorous applause] *This applies to all offices, civilian and military, at home.* [Shouts of 'Bravo', applause] *Perhaps this in itself will make the work of the various offices quicker and less cumber-some.* [Shouts of 'Bravo', enthusiastic applause] *In wartime we should work promptly, not just thoroughly. The soldier at the front doesn't have weeks to reflect at length on some measure,* [laughter] *and then pass on the folder from one person to the next* [laughter] *and then let the folder lie gathering dust.* [Laughter] *He must act at once or die! Here at home, we may not risk our own lives by working inefficiently, but we endanger the life of the Reich.*

Frivolous jobs in industry and the administration that have nothing to do with the war must also cease. [Shouts of 'Bravo'] *Many things that in peace-time were pleasant and worth doing seem ridiculous at the very least in war-time. When, for example, as I have heard, a whole string of offices in Berlin is occupied for weeks with the issue of whether the word 'accumulator' should be replaced by the word 'collector'* [laughter] *and numerous files are created on this subject,* [laughter] *my impression (which I believe is shared by the German*

*nation) is that people with such trivial concerns in wartime don't have enough
to do and would be more usefully employed in a munitions factory or at the
front!* [Enthusiastic agreement and applause]

*Everyone employed in the service of the nation must always be a shining
example to the nation, both in their work and in their outward bearing and
inner attitude. Even small matters can provoke public discontent. For example,
it's provocative for young men and women to ride on horseback through the
Tiergarten in Berlin at 9 o'clock in the morning.* [Indignation, applause] *I
sometimes wonder whether they'll coincide with a working-class woman who
has just done a ten-hour night shift and has to look after three, four, or five
children at home. Seeing a cavalcade gallop by as in peacetime can only cause
resentment in such a conscientious working woman.* [Shouts, applause] *I have
therefore banned horse riding on public roads and in public squares in the Reich
capital for the duration of the war.* [Shouts of 'Bravo', vigorous applause] *In
doing so I believe I am responding to the psychological requirements of the war*
[interjections] *and also to the need to consider the front. For example, a soldier on his way home on leave for a few days from the eastern front who stops
off for a day in Berlin will gain quite the wrong impression of our Reich capital
if he catches sight of such things!* [Indignant shouts] *Of course, he doesn't see
those hundreds of thousands of hard-working, decent men and women in the
armaments factories who work twelve-, fourteen-, and sometimes sixteen-hour
days but only a jolly company of indolent riders. What impressions of the homeland is he going to pass on later at the front! In these times every one of us must
accept unquestioningly the wartime rule that the greatest consideration should
be paid to the justified demands of the working and fighting population. We
aren't killjoys but we won't let anyone undermine our efforts.*

*It is, for example, a scandal that certain men and women lounge around for
weeks in spa resorts* [indignant shouts, applause], *picking up the latest gossip
and taking places from the seriously injured and working men and women who
after a year's arduous service are entitled to annual leave.* [Shouts of 'Shame']
We have put a stop to it. [Shouts of 'Bravo', enthusiastic applause] *Wartime
doesn't suit a certain kind of empty-headed riff-raff.* [Interjections] *Until the
war is over, work and struggle are where we find inner satisfaction. Anyone who
hasn't the sense of duty to understand that must be drilled in it and if necessary
coerced. Only a serious crackdown will work!* [Shouts of 'Bravo', applause]

*For example, the nation isn't impressed if we come out with the slogan 'Wheels
must turn for victory!' in a huge propaganda campaign and everyone takes note
and avoids unnecessary journeys, but the result is simply that unemployed leisure
travellers have more room on the train.* [Shouting] *The railways today are for*

transports vital to the war and for business travel necessary to the war! The only people who can lay claim to holidays are those whose ability to work or to serve in the military would otherwise be severely at risk. Since the outbreak of war and long before it the Führer hasn't had a single day off. If therefore the first man in the state takes such a serious and responsible view of his duty, then the unspoken and yet inescapable challenge to every citizen must be to follow his lead.

At the same time, the government is doing everything it can to preserve much-needed leisure facilities for the working population during this difficult period. Theatres, cinemas, music venues remain fully operational. Radio will work hard to extend and improve its range of programmes. We have no intention of shrouding the nation in a grey and wintry atmosphere. Whatever serves the nation, whatever preserves, strengthens, and increases its capacity to work and to fight is good and vital to the war effort. Anything that works against that must go. So to compensate for the measures I have just outlined, I have decreed that places promoting mental and psychological well-being that our Party comrade Ley is developing should not be reduced but rather increased. [Shouts of 'Bravo', applause]

The same goes for sport. Nowadays sport is not something only for the privileged classes. Exemptions from military service, by the way, are a nonsense in the realm of sport. [Shouts of 'Bravo'] *Sport exists to strengthen the body but chiefly so that that strength can be put to use during the worst emergency the nation has known.*

The front wants all of these things too. It calls with one voice on the German nation at home to stand in solidarity with it. We aim to do away with officiousness and pomposity that do not support the war. We refuse to spend any more time or money on them. We aim to do away with exaggerated and fussy form-filling for every little thing. We refuse to get bogged down in a thousand trivial matters that were perhaps important in peacetime but have no relevance to the war. We know now what we have to do. The German nation demands a Spartan existence for all, for high and low, rich and poor. Just as the Führer sets an example for the whole nation, so the whole nation, people of every rank, must make him their example. If he knows only work and cares, we will not leave him to work and worry alone but take upon ourselves the part that we can take off him.

For any true National Socialist, the period we are living through now bears an astonishing resemblance to the time of struggle. Then and ever since we have acted in the same way. We have always gone through thick and thin with the nation and that is why the nation has always been our liegeman. We have always borne every burden along with the nation and so these burdens don't seem heavy to us but light. The nation wants leadership! Throughout history the nation has never failed in its allegiance to a courageous and determined leader in a time of crisis.

[16] *I should like to say a few words in this regard about some practical measures relating to total war that we've already taken. The problem we're dealing with is how to free soldiers for the front and how to free workers for the armaments industry. All other needs must be subordinated to these two aims, even to the detriment of our society's standard of living during the war. This reduction in our standard of living should not be regarded as permanent, but only as a means to an end.*

As part of this effort hundreds of thousands of exemptions from military service at home must now be annulled. [Shouts of 'Bravo', enthusiastic applause] *These exemptions were necessary up to now because we lacked enough specialist and key workers to replace the vacancies arising if no exemptions were in force. The purpose of the measures taken and to be taken is to mobilize the labour necessary to do this. We are thus calling on all men who have hitherto not been part of the war economy and all women who have not been in the labour market. They will be unwilling, indeed unable, to turn a deaf ear to this appeal. The requirement for women to work is formulated in very broad terms. That does not mean, however, that only those who are specified in the law are allowed to work.* [Laughter] *We are glad of all help and the more women who join in this great process of redeployment in the domestic economy, the more soldiers we can free up for the front and the more vigorously the Führer can attack this summer!* [Shouts of 'Bravo', enthusiastic applause]

[17] *Our enemies claim that German women are incapable of replacing men in the war economy.* [Indignant murmurings] *That may be true of certain kinds of heavy physical work in our war production. But apart from that I'm convinced that German women are determined not just to do half the job of a man who goes to the front but the whole job, and in the shortest possible time.* [Enthusiastic applause] *We need not resort to bolshevist models. For years many millions of the finest German women have been working successfully in the war economy and they now look forward to new recruits joining them soon and swelling their ranks. All those who offer themselves for this work are doing no more than showing the proper gratitude due to those at the front. Hundreds of thousands have come forward. Hundreds of thousands more will do likewise. Very soon we hope to free up armies of workers who in their turn will free up armies of fighting men for the front!* [Shouts of 'Bravo', applause]

[16] Only in the last third of the speech does Goebbels address what are in fact the substantial measures required by 'total war', namely the large-scale redeployment that will release soldiers for the front as well as labour for the armaments industry. In addition to abolishing 'exemptions from military service', which led to some workers on the home front being declared 'essential' and not subject to conscription, the main objective here is to mobilize more female workers.

[17] In this section of his speech Goebbels, at times ironic and at times ostentatiously self-confident, takes issue with various concerns and difficulties that might obstruct any extension of women's work. He assures his audience that women are not to be employed doing heavy physical war work, but they themselves should not try to evade their duty to the fatherland, for example by producing medical certificates or taking up sham employment: 'egoistic, private needs' must take a back seat. Addressing the objection that by expanding women's work the regime was trying to copy bolshevism, he appears to make some concessions to the kinds of reservations found particularly among the middle classes about any expansion of women's work. The suggestion that people might do without a maid, or the comment that there were plenty of jobs that even women from a 'privileged background' could do, point unequivocally, however, to the real thrust of this passage.

[18] *I would have to be very wrong about German women if I assumed they would ignore this appeal. They will not stick in a mean-minded fashion to the letter of the law, let alone attempt to evade it altogether. I don't believe it. I can't imagine it. Besides, the few who act in this way will not cut any ice with us. Doctors' certificates* [loud murmurings] *will not be accepted.* [Laughter, vigorous applause] *Any so-called alibi work for a husband or brother-in-law or good friend that anyone acquires* [shouts of 'Bravo', applause] *in order to evade real work will meet with appropriate counter-measures.* [Murmurings, shouts of 'Bravo'] *The few who pursue such plans will only destroy their public reputation. We forget nothing and after the war we shall remember.* [Shouts of 'Bravo', applause] *People will regard them with the utmost contempt. Of course, no one is demanding that a woman who is physically incapable of it should do heavy duty work, for example in a tank factory. There are, however, many, many jobs in the war industry that do not require great physical effort, and a woman can do them, even if she comes from a privileged background.* [Approval, vigorous applause]

Women who employ servants should also give this matter careful consideration. [Murmurings, shouts of 'Bravo'] *They can perfectly well look after the household and children themselves and make the maid available for other work* [shouts of 'Yes', applause] *or—or hand over the household and children to the maid or the National Socialist Welfare§ and work themselves.* [Approving noises, applause] *Of course, life is then less cosy than in peacetime.* [Murmurs] *When Dad gets home, Mum is not always ready with the dinner.* [Laughter] *But we are not living in peacetime, we are at war! Cosiness is something we can enjoy when victory has been won.* [Shouts of 'Bravo', applause] *For the time being we must sacrifice comfort in order to gain victory!* [Shouting]

Soldiers' wives in particular will understand this. They will regard it as their highest duty to stand by their men at the front by offering themselves for vital war work. That's true above all in agriculture. The wives of agricultural workers can set a good example here. For men and women alike, the same principle holds: it isn't right for anyone to do less in wartime than in peacetime. More work must be done, not less.

It would, however, be wrong to leave it to the government to do everything that's necessary. The government can only create a broad framework of laws. It's the working population that must give them life and substance, and this will happen under the Party's inspiring leadership. [Hesitant applause] *Rapid action is of prime importance here.*

Over and above legal obligations, therefore, the watchword is: Volunteers, come forward!

§ Translators' note: Nationalsozialistische Volkswohlfahrt (NSV).

[18] The appeal he makes to women is therefore correspond-ingly long, for he is calling on the 'good name' that Berlin women in particular had earned, for 'national duty' and 'solidarity'. As these words make clear, even in times of national emergency, the use of women's labour, in particular in the armaments industry, was by no means taken for granted. Goebbels at any rate felt that additional 'persuasion' was needed. Incidentally, Magda Goebbels's plan to take up a job at Telefunken was never fulfilled, the reason given being her poor health.[13] As far as Goebbels's own sense of solidarity was concerned, during the war he main-tained three large households in Berlin (his official residence in the centre, the villa on Schwanenwerder, and the extensive estate in Lanke), plus a log cabin in Lanke that he used as a very private retreat, a second villa, the 'cavalier's house' on Schwanenwerder, to which he could also retreat, as well as an apartment in his ministry and another at his disposal in Rheydt Palace, in his birthplace of Rheydt. All this was somewhat in con-flict with the Spartan attitude he preached and demanded of others.

As Gauleiter of Berlin I'm appealing now to the women of Berlin, my fellow citizens. In the course of the war they have already offered so many noble examples of their courageous attitude that I feel sure they will want to respond to this request. Their practical approach and cheerful attitude to life even in wartime have aroused the admiration of the world. It's now time to build on this good name through generous action. If therefore I call on the women of Berlin as fellow citizens to offer themselves promptly, speedily, and unquestioningly for work vital to the war I know that they will all respond. [Applause] We're going—[Continued applause] We're going to stop complaining about the difficult times or grumbling to each other and instead we are going to get stuck in, to act, seize the initiative, do something ourselves and not leave everything to others. That's not just the Berlin way, it's the German way.

What German woman would have the heart to turn a deaf ear to such an appeal, made to all German women on behalf of the soldiers at the front? Who at this time would place a philistine concern for her own comfort above the call of national duty? Who, in the face of the severe threat we're all facing, would think of her egoistic, private needs and not of the overwhelming needs of the war?

I reject with contempt our enemies' accusation that we are copying bolshevism. We're not aiming to imitate bolshevism now any more than in the time of struggle. Rather, we are aiming to defeat it. German women will understand that soonest of all for they have long since realized that the war our men are fighting is above all a war to protect their children. The nation's most precious blood is defending women's most costly treasure. Now German women must demonstrate spontaneously and overtly their solidarity with the men's struggle. They must join the ranks of the millions of busy female employees and workers tomorrow rather than the day after and swell the army of workers on the home front. [Cry of 'To the front'] A surge of willingness must sweep through the German nation. I expect countless women and above all men who are not yet doing any vital war work to report to the registration offices. Those who offer themselves quickly offer themselves twice over.

[19] In addition, there will be a series of large-scale mergers across our economy, details of which have already appeared in the press. I know that many in our nation will be forced to make serious sacrifices. We acknowledge these sacrifices and our national leaders are at pains to keep them to a minimum. Nevertheless, there will unfortunately still be something of a burden for people to bear. After the war we shall build up everything we are dissolving today bigger and better than before, and the state will lend a helping hand.

I reject emphatically the claim that our measures are designed to shut down small, independent businesses or turn our economy into a monopoly. Immediately after the war small and medium-sized businesses will be fully active again and restored to their former position in society.

[19] Goebbels comes now to a further key element in his planned package of measures, namely to the 'large-scale mergers across our economy'. He is referring to the closure above all of smaller businesses. Here again he echoes the concerns felt by large sections of the middle class by rejecting the assertion that the intention was somehow to 'shut down small, independent businesses or turn our economy into a monopoly'. These were purely 'emergency measures', he says, and no 'change in the structure of the economy' was planned.

The present measures are exclusively emergency measures to support the war and its requirements. Their aim is not to bring about change in the structure of the economy, but merely to achieve total victory.

I don't dispute that carrying out the measures I have described will cause anxiety in the weeks ahead. But they will at last relieve the pressure on us. We are gearing these measures to the military action planned for this coming summer, and as we get to work we're disregarding the threats and boastfulness of the enemy. I am fortunate to be able to present this programme for victory to a German nation that is not only willing to take on these measures but positively demands them and indeed demands them more urgently than ever before in the course of this war. [Applause] The nation wants speedy and radical action. We have to make the most of this moment so that we're safe from unexpected developments in the future.

[20] In the past we've often appealed to the example of Frederick the Great in newspaper articles and speeches. We were not really entitled to do this. In the Third Silesian War Frederick II at times faced an enemy of 90 million, according to Schlieffen's reckoning, with 5 million Prussians. In the second of seven hellish years he suffered a defeat that rocked the entire Prussian state. He never had enough soldiers or weapons to fight his battles without enormous risk. His strategy was always one of stop-gap measures, but he stuck to the principle of attacking the enemy whenever the opportunity arose and beating him right where he was challenged. The fact that he suffered defeats was not crucial. What was crucial was that, whatever blows fate dealt him, this great king remained unbroken, that he steadfastly bore the vicissitudes of war, and his heart of iron overcame every danger. Though only fifty-one, at the end of the seven years he had become 'Old Fritz', a toothless old man, plagued by gout and countless other pains, but on the devastated battlefield he was the victor. What gives us the right to use him as an example? We simply want to summon up the strength of will and determination to act as he did, if need be. We too will remain unshakable whatever fate brings, and like him we shall try to wring victory even from the most adverse circumstances, never despairing of the great cause for which we fight.

[21] It's my deep conviction that the German nation has been purged and refined in its innermost being as a result of the blow fate dealt us at Stalingrad.

[20] Goebbels now changes abruptly to a historical perspective, focusing on the 'example of Frederick the Great'. After losing the Battle of Kunersdorf in the Seven Years' War 'Old Fritz' had found himself in a hopeless position but nevertheless had remained 'unbroken' and 'steadfast' and finally emerged from the war victorious.

In the previous years National Socialist propaganda had energetically cultivated the myth surrounding Frederick the Great, most recently in an extravagant feature film called 'The Great King', which highlighted Frederick's determination and endurance after defeat in battle. The film was released in spring 1942 and Goebbels had made use of the opportunity to compare Hitler with the Prussian king in a speech made on the occasion of Hitler's 53rd birthday: Was the latter, like his historical role model, not also engaged in a 'titanic struggle' for 'the life of our nation'?[14] In making the comparison Goebbels was initiating a change in the official propaganda surrounding 'the Führer', one that took account of the worsening war situation. The focus was no longer on the charisma of the successful national leader, statesman, and general, but on presenting Hitler as a heroic figure who, weighed down by heavy responsibilities, was doggedly fending off the threat of defeat. Consequently, propaganda could no longer present the 'Führer' as a conqueror cheered by the masses and omnipresent in the media. Rather, it faced the challenge of continuing to cultivate the mystique of a hero figure who was manifestly past his prime but whose leadership potential was alleged to be undiminished, while also factoring in that this figure had almost vanished from the public eye.

[21] Describing the German nation as having 'been purged and refined', Goebbels then attempts to present Stalingrad as a

It has stared war, cruel and pitiless, in the face. It now knows the unsparing truth and is determined to follow the Führer through thick and thin. [Shouts of 'Bravo', applause, interjections]

Loyal and trustworthy allies are standing by us. [Applause, shouts of 'Bravo'] *The Italian nation* [shouts of 'Bravo', enthusiastic applause] *under the leadership of its great 'Duce' will resolutely march with us towards victory.* [Shouts of 'Bravo', applause] *Fascist doctrine has made it mature enough to face all trials of fate. In East Asia the courageous Japanese nation* [shouts of 'Bravo', vigorous applause] *is landing blow upon blow on the Anglo-Saxon armed forces. Three major world powers along with their allies are leading the struggle against plutocratic tyranny. What can harm us if we submit with determination to the severe trials of this war? Our victory is not in doubt.* [Shouts of 'Bravo', vigorous and sustained applause] *While our fronts in the east fight their massive defensive battles against the hordes from the Steppe, our U boat war is raging across the oceans. The enemy's shipping is suffering losses that cannot remotely be offset by new and replacement vessels, however much their quantity is artificially boosted.* [Shouts of 'Bravo', applause] *Furthermore, this summer the enemy will see us on the offensive again!* [Noisy agreement and vigorous applause] *The German nation is determined to summon up all its energies to provide the Führer with the resources he needs.* [Shouts of 'Bravo', applause] *That's the task of this hour.*

[22] *I shall draw to a close.*

Recently a lot has appeared in the English and American press about the state of mind of the German nation in the present crisis. Clearly the boastful English know the German nation much better than we, its leaders. Hypocrites that they are, they give us advice on what to do, always under the mistaken impression that the German nation today is the same as the German nation of 1918 [shout of 'Never!'], *whereas in* 1918 *this nation was taken in by the deceit of the English. I needn't bother to produce arguments to prove them wrong. They're proved wrong every day by the way in which the German people are fighting and working.*

But, as a demonstration of the truth of this, I should like, German comrades, to put to you a series of questions that you must answer to the best of your knowledge and belief. When on 30 *January my audience spontaneously showed their approval of my demands, the next day the English–American (in other words the Jewish) press claimed it was a propaganda spectacle and in no way representative . . .* [indignant cries, shouts of 'Shame'] *and in no way representative of the true mood of the German nation, which the Jews know better than we do.* [Indignant cries] *Today I have invited a cross-section of the German nation as a whole in the truest sense of the word to this event. In front of me are rows of wounded soldiers from the eastern front* [thunderous applause], *men who have lost arms and legs . . .* [sustained and enthusiastic kind of moral self-purification. His subsequent praise for Germany's allies is uneven. Whereas he sees the Italian nation as being on the shared road to victory, he affirms, to somewhat more enthusiastic applause, that the 'courageous Japanese nation' is dealing their common enemies 'blow upon blow'.

[22] Before Goebbels puts his notorious ten questions to the audience at the end of his speech, he claims categorically that the crowd gathered in the Sports Palace is 'a cross-section of the German nation as a whole in the best sense of the word'. He is addressing the front-line soldiers and wounded who are present, as well as members of various professions, women, the young, the old, and so on, and he calls on his audience in the hall to confirm that 'a cross-section of the entire German nation both at the front and on the home front' is gathered there. He does, though, add the qualification that 'Jews . . . are not represented here', which elicits thunderous applause and shouts of 'Jews out!'. As responses to the event will show, however, this attempt by Goebbels to declare those present (in essence the usual National Socialist activists who regularly attended Sports Palace rallies) authentic representatives of the German nation, thereby elevating the subsequent question-and-answer gimmick to the status of a plebiscite, is an all too transparent propaganda trick.

applause] *arms and legs, men who have been blinded and have come with their Red Cross nurses, men in their prime whose crutches are propped up in front of them. Among them I can count some fifty men wearing the Oak Leaves and the Knight's Cross* [shouts of 'Heil', enthusiastic applause, shouting], *brilliant representatives of our fighting men at the front!* [Applause] *Behind them is a block of armaments workers from Berlin armoured vehicle factories!* [Loud shouts, enthusiastic applause] *Behind them are Party officials, front-line soldiers from the Wehrmacht, doctors, academics, artists, engineers and architects, teachers, civil servants and officials, a proud cross-section of our intellectual life at every level, to which the Reich now in wartime owes miracles of inventiveness and human genius.* [Hesitant applause] *I see thousands of German women right round the Sports Palace.* [Shouts of 'Bravo', applause] *There are young people here as well as old. Every social group, every trade and profession, and every age group was included in the invitation. I am therefore fully justified in saying: The people sitting in front of me are a cross-section of the entire German nation both at the front and on the home front! Am I right?* [Shouts of 'Yes', audible agreement and enthusiastic applause] *Jews, it must be said, are not represented here!* [Loud applause, shouts of 'Jews out!']

[23] *At this moment, therefore, you, my audience, represent the nation as far as the world outside Germany is concerned, and I should like to put ten questions to you that you, along with the German nation, must answer before the whole world, but especially before our enemies, who are listening in on their radios at this very moment. Are you willing?* [Loud shouts of 'Yes']

The English claim the German nation has lost its faith in victory. [Noisy dissent, great agitation]

I ask you: Do you believe with the Führer and with us in the final total victory of German arms? [Enthusiastic agreement, many shouts of 'Sieg Heil']

I ask you: Are you determined to follow the Führer through thick and thin to achieve this victory, accepting even the heaviest personal cost? [A loud 'Yes', enthusiastic agreement, great excitement, many shouts of 'Sieg Heil']

Second: The English claim the German nation is tired of fighting. [Shouts of 'No', noisy disagreement]

I ask you: Are you prepared, as the home phalanx standing behind the armed forces in the field, to continue fighting alongside the Führer unswervingly and with fierce determination through every twist and turn of fate until victory is ours? [Loud cries of 'Yes', demonstrative bursts of applause]

Third: The English claim the German nation is unwilling to accept the increasing burden of war work required by the government. [Indignant objections]

I ask you, soldiers and workers, if the Führer should command it in an emergency, are you and the German nation determined to work ten, twelve, if

[23] First of all, Goebbels secures the audience's consent to his question-and-answer ritual ('Are you willing?'). He then introduces each of the ten questions with 'I ask you', prefacing each of the first five with an alleged claim made by 'English' propaganda about 'the German nation'. Like the speech as a whole, this list of questions is designed to reach a climax.

In questions one to three, which overlap in content, Goebbels prompts the audience to affirm its belief in victory and its readiness to commit all to achieving victory, so that its enthusiastic assent to the fourth question, the question about 'total war', will give him a sort of interim result. Question five consolidates this by testing the audience on its unlimited confidence in the Führer, a component already of questions one to three.

After Goebbels has thus committed his audience to the implementation of 'total war' in concrete terms, he uses questions six to ten to win their assent to a complete commitment to weapons production. In addition, they accept the home front's unconditional support for the front, the mobilization of women, severe punishments for 'shirkers and black-marketeers', and solidarity in the distribution of 'rights' and 'duties'.

need be fourteen or sixteen hours a day, and give your all for victory? [Passionate cries of 'Yes', applause]

Fourth: *The English claim the German nation is resisting the measures the government is taking towards total war.* [Indignant shouts] *It does not want total war, the English say, but rather capitulation.* [Noisy opposition, shouts of 'Never!']

I ask you: Do you want total war? [Shouts of 'Yes' and enthusiastic and sustained applause, shouting] *If necessary, do you want a war more total and radical than we can possibly imagine today?* [Shouts of 'Yes', applause]

Fifth: *The English claim the German nation has lost faith in the Führer.* [Indignant shouting, muddled shouts, uproar, shouts of 'Sieg Heil']

I ask you... [chants of 'Führer, command us, we shall follow you!', shouts of 'Heil'] *I ask you: Do you have faith in the Führer?* [Storm of agreement] *Are you willing absolutely and unconditionally to follow him wherever he leads and to do everything necessary to bring the war to a victorious end?* [Shouts of 'Yes']

I ask you this sixth question: Are you ready from now on to devote all your strength to provide the eastern front, our fathers and brothers who are fighting, with the manpower and the weapons they need to defeat bolshevism? [Shouts of 'Yes', enthusiastic applause, random shouts]

I ask you this seventh question: Do you give your most solemn oath to the front that the homeland stands behind it, its morale high and unshakable, and will give it anything it needs for victory? [Shouts of 'Yes', enthusiastic applause]

I ask you this eighth question: Are you willing—and I ask you women in particular—for the government to ensure that every last worker, women included, is used to support the war [individual shouts of 'Yes'] *and that wherever possible women should fill jobs that will free up men for the front? Do you want this?* [Shouts of 'Yes', enthusiastic applause]

I ask you this ninth question: Do you approve, if necessary, of the most radical measures against a small number of shirkers and black-marketeers [shouts of 'Yes', continued shouting] *who pretend in the midst of war that it is peacetime and exploit the nation's distress for selfish ends?* [Cries of 'String them up!', shouting] *Do you agree that anyone who abuses the conditions of wartime should lose his head?* [Shouts of 'Yes', enthusiastic applause]

And now my tenth and final question: In this time of war, do you want equal rights and equal duties to apply to everyone, as prescribed in the National Socialist Party programme? [Shouts of approval] *Do you want the home front to bear the same heavy burdens of the war in solidarity with the front, and those burdens to be shared equally by high and low and rich and poor? Do you want this?* [Shouts of 'Yes', thunderous applause]

I have put my questions and you have freely given your answers. You are a part of the nation and have given voice to the nation's view. [Shouts] *You have shouted out to our enemies what they need to know so that they harbour no illusions or false ideas.* [Various shouts]

[24] *And now we are firmly united in brotherhood with the German nation, as we have been from the moment we came to power and through all these last ten years. The most powerful ally in the world, the nation itself, is behind us and determined to fight for victory with the Führer, whatever the cost and ready to accept even the most painful sacrifices!* [Shouts of 'Bravo', enthusiastic applause]

I stand here before you not only as a spokesman for the government but also as a spokesman for the nation. My old friends from the Party, who hold high offices as leaders of the nation and the state, are sitting round me. Party comrade Speer is sitting next to me. [Shouts of 'Heil', applause] *The Führer has given him the historic mission of mobilizing the German armaments industry and supplying the front with all the weapons it needs. Party comrade Dr Ley* [shouts of 'Heil', applause] *is sitting next to me. The Führer has given him the task of leading the German labour force and training and educating them to carry out their war duties tirelessly. We are indebted to Party comrade Sauckel whom the Führer has given the task* [rising applause] *of bringing countless thousands of workers into the Reich. In addition, all leaders of the Party, the Wehrmacht, and the state are united with us.*

[25] *We all are children of our nation, welded together with the nation at the most critical hour in our national history. We vow to you and to the front, we vow to the Führer that we shall forge from the home front a single and concentrated will on which the Führer and his fighting men can rely absolutely and unquestioningly.* [Shouts of 'Bravo', enthusiastic applause] *We commit ourselves to do anything necessary, at home or at work, to achieve victory. We shall fill our hearts with that political passion, an ever-burning fire that in the great periods of struggle as a Party and a state always consumed us. In this war we shall never fall prey to those false and hypocritical delusions about objectivity that have brought the German nation so much misfortune in its history.*

When this war began we fixed our gaze solely on the nation. Whatever serves it and its struggle to survive is good and must be preserved and promoted. Whatever harms it and its struggle is bad and must be removed and cut off. We shall approach the task of overcoming the great problems of this phase of the war with passionate hearts and cool heads. Thus we shall be set for final victory. That victory is founded on faith in the Führer! [Shouts of 'Heil', enthusiastic applause] *He expects us to perform in a way that puts all past achievements in the shade. We shall not fail to meet his challenge. We are proud of him and will make him proud of us.*

[24] In his concluding appeal Goebbels begins by giving his own summing-up of the question-and-answer ritual: 'You...have given voice to the nation's view.' It is the nation itself that, whatever the cost, intends to stand with the 'Führer' and fight for victory, he says. He then stresses the National Socialist leadership's strong connection with the nation and briefly refers to Speer, Ley, and Sauckel, who are present at the rally.

[25] There follow a vow made to the 'front' and the 'Führer' to stand together unconditionally, an appeal to 'political passion', and a rejection of any 'false and hypocritical delusions about objectivity'—a statement always wheeled out in Nazi propaganda when it wanted to prevent any rational evaluation of the arguments. After again invoking the certainty of victory and adding yet one more profession of loyalty to the 'Führer', he chooses as his concluding sentence a line adapted from a poem by Theodor Körner, famous in his day for writing political poems at the time of the Wars of Liberation from Napoleonic rule. Goebbels alludes here unmistakably to the call to national mobilization issued by the kingdom of Prussia in 1813 in its war against the French occupiers. Only a few months later Goebbels will task the film director Veit Harlan with making an 'epic' that begins with this very call to arms by the still hesitant king and uses the resistance of the citizens of the Prussian city of Kolberg against Napoleon's conquering army as a historical model of heroic struggle.

The rally closes with the national anthem and the Horst Wessel Song.

It is in the great crises and tribulations of national life that true men show their worth, and true women too. No one has a right to talk of the weaker sex any more, for both sexes demonstrate the same fierce fighting spirit and inner strength. The nation is ready for this. The Führer has commanded and we shall follow him. If we have ever believed loyally and unswervingly in victory, then we do so now in this moment of national reflection and inner resolve. It is within our grasp and we have only to reach out for it! We need only summon the determination to subordinate everything to this goal. That is the order of the day. And so from now on the watchword is:

Nation, arise, and let the storm break forth! [Shouts of 'Heil' and applause, chants of 'Sieg Heil']

3

After the speech

The day after the speech Goebbels recorded his impressions of the event in his diary: 'The atmosphere among the people was one of wild frenzy. The audience was made up of all social classes, from the government down to the anonymous munitions worker.' Carried away by his own success, he evidently overlooked the fact that he himself had seen to it that the audience was carefully composed of members of the NSDAP. Goebbels went on: 'My speech left an indelible impression. Even at the start it was being continuously interrupted by thunderous applause. The audience's reaction was indescribable. The Sports Palace has never witnessed such uproar as at the end, when I put my ten questions to the audience. They were answered with storms of approval.'

He professed himself convinced that the event would 'make a profound impression not only on the Reich but also on neutral foreign countries and even on enemy ones'. Almost 'the whole of the Reich cabinet, any number of Reichsleiters and Gauleiters, and almost all the state secretaries' had been present: 'In brief, this rally represented a cross-section of the entire German nation. I was, I believe, in excellent form as an orator and worked the assembled audience up into a something like a state of total mental mobilization. The close of the rally was a wild hullabaloo.' Politically his conclusion was thus clear: 'As this rally proves, the nation is prepared to offer up everything for the war and for victory. Now we just need to make the most of it.'[1]

After the event Goebbels invited a number of the prominent members of the audience to a party at his villa and convinced himself that influential figures such as Göring's state secretary Milch, Speer, Ley, Stuckart, state secretary at the Interior Ministry, Justice Minister Thierack, or Körner, state secretary responsible for the Four-Year Plan, were on his side. He told himself he should really organize such occasions more frequently in order to consolidate 'a certain leadership position for the

Gauleiter of Berlin'. This was 'absolutely necessary, as the Führer's absence from Berlin means that there is actually no central political leadership'.[2]

He was even very taken with the reaction of his two daughters. Both Hilde and Helga had been 'deeply impressed': 'Helga in particular, though she didn't understand everything in my speech, was deeply affected by the experience. I'm pleased that our children, young as they are, are having an introduction to politics.' Everything had therefore gone according to plan and he summed up the day thus:

During the evening the view was frequently expressed that this rally represents a kind of silent coup d'état. We have simply leapt over all the hurdles set up by bureaucracy to block us. Total war is now no longer a cause espoused by a few perceptive men but has been embraced by the whole nation.

In the days that followed, Goebbels became positively intoxicated by the responses of the media at home and abroad. The speech had been 'a first-rate sensation and is filling the headlines and the front pages of virtually all the newspapers in the world'. The most substantial comments, he noted with pride, 'are from friendly and allied countries', which was, after all, hardly surprising. He had also achieved 'huge resonance', he claimed, in a number of neutral states. From the regular telephone surveillance of journalists from these countries based in Berlin, he saw evidence that these circles were also extremely impressed. On the evening of the 19 February, as he stated, 'the response to my speech is swelling to gigantic proportions'. If he had dismissed the first polemical reactions from Great Britain as 'empty phrases and bits of snot', he now claimed that 'the initial inanities in London' had been 'quickly abandoned' and the speech was being acknowledged there as being 'one of the greatest achievements of war propaganda' in general; the 'thunderous applause' had, according to Swedish correspondents in London, 'attracted the greatest attention'.[3] His elation at his own success lasted through the next two days: The speech was still dominating 'the headlines of the great newspapers across the world' and had left the most 'profound impression' above all in neutral states.[4]

These comments are glaring examples of how completely the German Propaganda Minister misread the international response to his speech. A detailed survey of the reaction of the foreign press makes this even clearer.[5]

The sensation that never was: reactions in the foreign press

The fact that not only the Spanish press[6] but above all the Italian[7] and that of the other allied states praised the speech to the skies and presented it in a way that fitted in with the Propaganda Ministry's line is hardly surprising, though that did not prevent Goebbels from expressing his deep satisfaction numerous times.[8]

Superficially the reactions from Switzerland were also extraordinarily positive. The most important Swiss papers carried a relatively detailed account of the speech, while the *Basler Nachrichten* and *Die Tat* even printed the text in full. In their fairly detailed comment on the content the papers made it particularly clear that the speech was to be understood as a response to a serious crisis, thus stressing the gravity of the situation the 'Third Reich' evidently found itself in. In addition, the Swiss papers, which in the main had correspondents on the spot in Berlin, reported on the immediate impact of the speech there. The *Baseler National-Zeitung* and *Die Weltwoche* in particular emphasized Goebbels's rhetorical achievement: The commentator in the *National-Zeitung* expressed the view that with this speech Goebbels had written himself into the 'annals of history', while the *Weltwoche* claimed it had been a 'masterpiece of propaganda' that showed 'the little doctor ever more clearly to be the real guiding hand behind the German home front'. The Berlin correspondent of *Die Tat* took the view that the speech had had its intended effect and 'galvanized' the German nation. On 19 February the liberal paper *Der Bund*, published in Berne, carried a detailed report on the speech, including long quotations, on page 2. The following day its comment was objective: The speech could be regarded as a call for a 'second revolution'.[9]

On 19 February the *Neue Zürcher Zeitung*, which had focused considerable attention in the days previously on the German measures for 'total war', gave prominence to the speech on the front page of its midday edition and also printed a report from its Berlin correspondent.[10]

If Goebbels felt flattered by this recognition of his oratorical skill and wrote elatedly in his diary of the 'warm sympathy' of the Swiss newspapers,[11] he completely failed to see that the concentrated focus on him as an individual defeated the intended purpose of the event. For his main objective in mounting it had been to create the impression

that the 'voice of the nation' had been demanding 'total war' and that
on 18 February he had merely revealed this fundamental determination to make the ultimate sacrifice and documented it (and had not
just then created it). But the Swiss press did not buy this line. Their
general assumption was that the event, though brilliantly prepared and
staged, was unmistakably a propaganda exercise. For example, the
Berlin correspondent of the *Neue Zürcher Zeitung* wrote that the composition of the audience showed that 'care had been taken to make the
event as representative as possible', thus revealing, albeit in a polite way,
the intention to create a false impression.[12]

   It is striking that elsewhere in neutral countries a series of extremely
critical views were expressed. The Turkish daily *Cumhuriyet*, for example,
followed up an initial report on 19 February with a comment piece
two days later: 'However much Goebbels would like to incite hatred
on the part of the European nations and England towards Russia and
bolshevism, their primary and unwavering aim will still be to defeat
Germany.' On 20 February *Yeni Sabah*, published in Istanbul, which
had also printed extracts from the speech on 19 February, disputed the
threat to the whole of Europe from bolshevism that Goebbels had
conjured up with such intensity; rather, it said, the greatest threat came
from Germany itself and people simply had to recognize that 'all statements in German propaganda are lies'. A further comment piece the
following day took the view that the Germans' confidence in Hitler
must have been shaken or else such an event would not have been
necessary. In addition, the commentator was completely unimpressed
by the orgy of cheering in Berlin: 'A nation whose conscience and
reason have been silenced and which is duty-bound to obey its leaders
blindly has no opportunity to express its (true) opinion.'[13]

   The Swedish press[14] too was overwhelmingly critical in its comments. In particular the *Göteborgs Handels- och Sjöfatstidning* (*Gothenburg
Financial and Maritime Newspaper*), which in general took a critical view
of Sweden's policy of neutrality, published an extremely pointed and
critical article on 19 February. In it the suspicion was expressed that
the audience in the Sports Palace had been carefully selected and the
conclusion posed the rhetorical question: 'Did those assembled not
express the Nazis' desire for self-preservation more than anything
else?' It is furthermore striking that the newspaper *Aftonbladet* quoted
Goebbels as saying their aim was the 'complete extermination of the
Jews', in other words not sticking to the written version of the speech

disseminated by the German News Agency, in which this passage had been changed.

Above all the British and American press were much less impressed by the speech than Goebbels was prepared to admit. It did not 'dominate the headlines' there in any way.

The 19 February edition of *The Times*, for example, carried its New York correspondent's laconic single-column report on the main points of the speech.[15] The same day the *Daily Express, Daily Herald*, and the *Daily Telegraph and Morning Post* each contained a single column on page 2 (the last of these with a continuation on page 6); the *Manchester Guardian's* report was somewhat more detailed, though only on page 5.

The *New York Times* for 19 February gave a summary of the speech on the front page (though without a headline) and then on page 8 quoted from it at length, the only well-known newspaper on the Allied side to do so.[16] This was followed two days later by a comment piece on an inside page that took issue with Goebbels in an ironic tone, concluding that the idea that Germany was playing an honourable role in the defence of Europe was simply pitiful.[17] On 19 February the *New York Herald Tribune* published a single-column report on the speech on pages 1 and 5 and presented it in a leading article the following day as the Propaganda Minister's usual tissue of lies.

On 19 February the *Washington Post* gave a summary in a double column on the front page, with a continuation on page 4.[18] Two days later a detailed comment piece appeared in the inside pages that surmised (misunderstanding Goebbels) that the speech was primarily a rejection of any hopes of peace being entertained in Germany and represented in particular a response to a leading article from 17 February by Virginio Gayda, the editor of the *Giornale d'Italia* and close friend of Mussolini. This article had been interpreted in some parts of the international press as the Italian government putting out covert feelers for peace negotiations.[19] Other news outlets also made similar connections between Gayda's article and Goebbels's speech,[20] much to the latter's annoyance, for he inevitably saw these comments as a distraction from his real message.[21]

The *San Francisco Chronicle* published two articles that took the speech as the prelude to a campaign for peace and/or (very perceptively) as the expression of an internal power struggle within the German leadership. The Baltimore *Evening Sun* dismissed the speech on 19 February on page 3 as a carefully rehearsed hysterical propaganda demonstration, and the same day the *Boston Daily Globe* published a short notice about the speech and on page 4 presented it as an expression of the German government's despair. Other leading US newspapers noted the speech in short reports or editorials.[22]

To sum up, in contrast to the reporting in Switzerland, further away from Berlin the 'plebiscite' on 'total war' provided by the audience in the Sports Palace on behalf of the nation was not at the forefront of international interest. Instead, the all too obvious demonstration of loyalty to Hitler was interpreted as a propaganda ploy and thus as a clear indication that confidence in the leadership was on the wane. As a result, reports mainly concentrated dispassionately on the text of the speech itself: on the deadly seriousness of the situation that came through, on the ramping up of the demands being made on the German population, and on the announcement that the occupied territories would be plundered even more ruthlessly. Read this way, the call for 'total war' seemed above all to be proof of a profound crisis within the German leadership and as a desperate attempt to find a way out. Commentators underlined the huge difference between swaggering announcements from Goebbels earlier on and this new tone. Besides this, 'Dr Goebbels', as the Allied press also liked to call him, was regarded as the incarnation of mendacity and his statements generally met with an ironical response.

The response in Germany

Goebbels described reactions in the press at home also as 'very strong'; his speech had been presented 'in fantastic style and with brilliant comment'. His narcissism was evidently so pronounced that he could ignore the fact that both presentation and comment had been ordered by his own ministry. On 20 February he also quoted in his diary with great pride a report of his Reich Propaganda Offices, confirming to their supreme boss that his 'propaganda had elicited the most profound response since 1932'. Later that evening he was 'very happy' on receipt of telegrams from Colonel General Dietl and General Field Marshal Richthofen, believing he could infer from them that the speech had been 'a wake-up call for the front'.[23]

In the days that followed we hear more of the same: 'The impact of the speech at home is huge'. He naturally seemed particularly gratified by Hitler's positive response: 'He has now studied my speech and all the accompanying material carefully and is deeply impressed by the success of the Sports Palace rally. He is describing this speech as a psychological and propagandistic tour de force first class.'[24]

The most recent Security Service report did not, however, chime in so well with this positive mood. Although it provided no detail as yet on his speech, its one-sided compilation of 'gripes' may, in Goebbels's view, have downplayed the change of mood the speech had brought about. A week after the speech Goebbels greeted the Security Service report of 22 February all the more warmly as 'its comments' had taken full account of 'my Sports Palace speech'. In spite of its positively shocking candour, the report said, 'the effect of the speech' had in the end been 'extraordinarily uplifting.... Total war now has the assent and support of the whole nation'.

A closer look at the Security Service report[25] reveals, however, that in his prolonged euphoria over his great feat Goebbels had overlooked the critical undertones of this document or else did not take them seriously. The Security Service had emphasized the wide dissemination of the speech and described its impact as 'unusually big and over all very favourable'. The 'national comrades', anxious after the most recent reports of further reverses on the eastern front, 'were positively longing for a clear account of the situation'. 'In spite of its very candid description of the seriousness of the situation', the speech had therefore 'eased tension and renewed confidence and trust in the war leadership'. The speaker, it said, had successfully generated 'enthusiasm and the atmosphere of the time of struggle' and this had communicated itself to the radio listeners too.

After the general commendation contained in these opening remarks, the detailed comments did, however, contain criticism. Thus the argument that there was an 'imminent threat' 'confirmed fears that the eastern front had not yet been stabilized, that the series of setbacks was not yet over, and that the war could still take a number of turns for the worse'. Many people had only just come to see the 'terrible seriousness of the situation'. Though fundamentally grateful for candour, many people now wished to be given more details about the military situation.

'Some individuals' had also taken the view that Goebbels had painted a 'blacker' picture of the situation 'than was really the case in order to give greater emphasis to the totalization measures', that his comments did not go beyond the 'already familiar measures and ideas', and that there was still talk of total war being implemented 'too late'. Though his announcement of the 'most radical enforcement of these measures' had 'everywhere elicited great approval', there remained 'doubts that they would be implemented equitably across all strata of society'.

The report thus came to the conclusion that Goebbels's unvarnished account of the situation and his call for increased war efforts had been understood also as an admission of failures both in the management of news and in the conduct of the war in general. Moreover, he had raised expectations that many were already convinced would never be fulfilled. The Security Service's evaluation made one thing very clear: The conscious break with the whole method of waging war up to that point that Goebbels intended his speech to introduce resulted also in some scope emerging for the expression of a wide spectrum of critical views. Thus the regime was relinquishing some of its rigid control of the public sphere.

The last part of the speech, the list of questions, had, according to the Security Service report, 'had a mixed reception'. Although 'in general the impact of the ten questions' had been emphasized, nevertheless 'national and Party comrades from all parts of society' had expressed the view that 'audience and readers had been too aware of the propagandistic aim of these questions and answers'. The report in other words made it very clear that there was a widespread view that Goebbels's entire performance with its recurring theme of 'Look: The nation is calling for "total war"' represented an all too transparent piece of propaganda theatre.

Above all, the Security Service report as a whole made it plain that radio and other media had not successfully communicated the impact of this piece of Berlin propaganda theatre to the population as a whole. To put it bluntly, the speech neither released a storm of approval across the land nor did it provoke any kind of uniform response at all. Though approving voices could be heard, it also provoked fear, criticism, and doubt. In addition, from among the regime's 'reports on the mood', five survive from Bavarian District Presidents who observed the 'situation and mood' in the area for which they were responsible throughout the entire duration of the 'Third Reich'. Like the Security Service report discussed above, all five begin by emphasizing the positive impact that 'Dr Goebbels's grand Sports Palace speech' has had; it made, they say, 'a deep impression', inspired 'courage and determination', was 'received in a spirit of trust' and had 'persuaded' and 'galvanized every last person'.[26]

At the same time, however, most of the reports contained numerous criticisms. In Lower Bavaria and in the Upper Palatinate the speech was said to have created 'real fear' in part of the audience and had confirmed the general 'conviction that from now on the population wants to be informed in candid and unvarnished terms about the situation'. This choice of words strongly suggested criticism of the official system of withholding and manipulating information.

The District President of Lower Franconia wrote of the speech that 'for people of a nervous disposition it was shocking because its unsparing candour left us in no doubt as to our perilous situation'. His opposite number in Swabia stated that the speech had 'provoked criticism and annoyance in many parts of society. The question: "Do you want the war to be even more total and radical than we can possibly imagine today?" was interpreted by many as meaning that hostilities will ultimately end in the use of gas.' And from Upper and Middle Franconia the view was: 'It was assumed that Part 2 (the questions to the audience) was unlikely to have made a striking impression abroad.' It was therefore altogether evident here, as in the Security Service report, that the question-and-answer orgy, which was supposed to demonstrate the complete harmony between nation and leadership, was seen as more or less transparently orchestrated.

From the judiciary, which maintained its own system of reporting on 'mood and attitude' in the population, there was also clear critical comment. On 19 March the President of the Higher Regional Court in Bamberg noted the prevailing reaction in his jurisdiction: 'In particular, the conclusion of the speech (question and answer) met with almost universal disapproval.' While people generally regarded the measures planned to achieve total war as necessary, they were 'keeping a beady eye on whether the implementation was rational and impartial'.[27]

His colleague from Zweibrücken who, though a Party member since the end of 1933, cannot be categorized as 'a typical National Socialist lawyer', couched his report in such terms as to make it read for long stretches like an explicit criticism of Goebbels's speech.[28] Of course, the measures in train were in principle necessary, as the president of the court at first emphasized, yet it was 'a consequence of the tensions and antagonisms caused by the long duration of the war that the desire of certain circles to see so-called "fine ladies" working in a factory did not spring from a concern to maximize German war potential but from other, less rational reasons'. It was important not to 'give women occupations for which they are physically unsuited purely for the look of the thing'.

In saying this the Zweibrücken judge was of course directly questioning the argument about the 'optics of the war' that Goebbels had just used to justify many of the planned measures. He had had reports, he goes on, that 'labour exchanges and Party offices' were being 'inundated at the moment with anonymous letters and others with hate-filled content'. 'Very astute, sure-footed, and firm management' would be required 'to lead and not be influenced by the instincts of the mob'. 'Class hatred' at any rate was 'still alive and particularly so given the mood of heightened resentment arising from the war. This is demonstrated by the fact that applause at public speeches never erupts with greater frenzy than when the so-called well-to-do' are the object of criticism. The senior judge added by way of warning: 'The instincts that are unleashed here can turn in a quite different direction.' To his mind, therefore, Goebbels's appeal to the absolute solidarity of the 'national community' had instead had the effect of dividing the population.

Even in the reporting of the Reich propaganda offices in the individual Gaus, which were subordinate to Goebbels's ministry, some notes of criticism were heard—in complete contrast to the altogether positive impression that Goebbels recorded in his diaries about the reports. Here too we read that among public servants and the upper classes there was criticism of the speech's pronounced notes of 'class conflict'; in Pomerania and in the Westphalia North Gau the event was described as pure propaganda and even expressly referred to as 'theatre'; in Swabia and Saxony Goebbels's claim that the positive responses to his ten questions should be regarded as a kind of plebiscite was considered implausible.[29]

Just how unwelcome such impressions were to those leading the ministry is shown by a circular of 27 February from its state secretary Leopold Gutterer to the Reich propaganda offices. In it he says he does not wish to receive reports detailing very negative attitudes among the population; such attitudes were to be eliminated with the 'methods of the time of struggle', in other words by the use of force. The circular made specific reference to a report from Saxony that higher education students had reacted negatively to the speech, although it had 'galvanized the entire nation, got Europe moving, and left our enemies the world over amazed at German strength'.[30] What is nevertheless becoming very clear is that, from the point of view of those at the top of the ministry, the process of gathering information on the population's mood by no means served as a tool of precise opinion research. Rather, its purpose lay first and foremost in reinforcing the desired propaganda effect through positive feedback.

The lack of consistency in the population's response, already highlighted in the reports on the public mood, can also be illustrated by means of extracts from diaries and letters, even if they cannot of course provide a representative picture of 'German' responses to the speech.

Convinced National Socialists and adherents of the regime mainly welcomed the measures announced. Thus Oberleutnant Heiner Grub, in civilian life a forestry official, wrote from the eastern front to his family on 20 February that he hoped:

the speeches of the last few days fulfilled their purpose at home. The complaining and grumbling just could not go on and it was high time that those in high places spoke out in terms that made it clear to everyone exactly what is at stake here and that this war concerns the whole nation and not just the soldiers. If people at home grasp this, it's a big step forward.[31]

Hertha Neureiter from Memmingen appeared similarly persuaded of the value of the measures announced, writing to her relatives: 'That's how it has to be. Dr G. is getting everything moving. Let's hope things will be done thoroughly and the front strengthened. It must end at some point. We can't go on like this.'[32]

Margarete Liebel, a young woman strongly influenced by National Socialism, wrote to her future husband immediately after hearing the speech on the radio of again feeling strongly her old impulse 'finally to be fully involved in the war effort'. She even considered giving up her training as an agriculture teacher shortly before her final examinations: 'For a long time now I haven't been able to see our studies as important to the war. What good will it do us to have a new generation with detailed professional training if in the meantime we lose the war?'[33] In the end, however, she did sit the 'state exam for teachers of agricultural household management' the following month and went on to take up a post.[34]

Even though the three examples above predominantly express approval of 'total war', in all three cases Goebbels's speech seems to have provoked a certain resentment at government failures.

For opponents of the regime the speech was first and foremost a transparent piece of propaganda theatre that was supposed to disguise the fact that the 'Third Reich' had reached a point where its war policy was obviously a complete failure. Their criticisms then led into a whole series of other observations.

Friedrich Kenner, for example, a court inspector from Laubach in Hesse and a former Social Democrat, recorded in his diary on 19 February:

In order to justify total war Reich Minister Dr Goebbels was let loose on the public on 18 February 1943 in the Berlin Sports Palace. Goebbels had seen to it that the composition of the massed audience guaranteed from the outset an 'enthusiastic' rally. Using all rhetorical means, he summoned up the spectre of bolshevism to frighten simple-minded citizens. He was using a very old weapon of the Nazis. Before 1933 their habit of whipping up fear of communists had great success. Now Goebbels believes he can deceive the whole world, not just Germany, with his arguments.[35]

Lengthy musings follow on the contradictory policies of the National Socialists, who had made a pact with Stalin in 1939 and then, by invading the Soviet Union two years later, had themselves mobilized on the Soviet side the 'enormous powers of resistance of the entire nation'. At the end Kellner focused on the concluding lines of the speech: 'Nation, arise! That would indeed be the right thing to do, but not in order to extend the war but to put an immediate stop to this insane war!'

The journalist Ruth Andreas-Friedrich, active in the resistance to the regime, took issue with Goebbels's comparative and superlative, 'Total—more total—most total': 'Anyone who is inwardly insecure must no doubt rely on such devices and struggle from one exaggerated expression to the next.... "If you're talking big, you need this," as the proverb goes. If that's true then the Nazis must really need it. Not only the most total war but the most total exertions to win this war.'[36]

Matthias Joseph Mehs from Wittlich, a deeply committed democrat and before 1933 one of the leading politicians of the Centre Party, recorded in his diary on 18 February that Goebbels (after his articles in *Das Reich* and the 30 January address) had come up with 'nothing new', but had said it 'very loudly, as if someone were holding a knife to his throat'. 'He seems to have sought permission to do this from the Berlin public, in other words an audience of invited guests and prominent Party members. So a Berlin National Socialist is representative of the whole of Germany.' On the ten questions Mehs wrote that 'in future' people would 'fail to understand how at such a critical time a representative of the government could employ such stupid gimmicks and how the people could just accept it like sheep. Our opponents will be laughing up their sleeves. Dr Goebbels has served the enemy better than his own nation.'[37]

Victor Klemperer, who because of his Jewish background had lost his post as Professor of Romance Literature at the Technical University in Dresden and only avoided deportation because he was married to a non-Jewish wife (he was under no illusions about the fate of those deported), was able to get hold of a newspaper with the text of the speech. He was of course struck most of all by Goebbels's threat to proceed against the Jews 'with the most draconian and radical means possible', but he also noted that the speech clearly showed the government threatening 'even "national comrades"'.[38]

In his diary entry for 19 February the Protestant army chaplain Siegfried Hotzel called the speech 'a masterpiece of unscrupulous demagoguery and suggestive manipulation of the masses'. It had seemed to him as if 'a mob of idiots and escaped lunatics had gathered there'.[39]

In the case of contemporaries who cannot be clearly identified as supporters or opponents of the regime the speech provoked very varied reactions. Quite a few were moved to reflections that conflicted with Goebbels's intentions. Thus Wilfried Nordmann, an artillery lieutenant, expressed surprise in his diary that 'in contrast to his overoptimistic stance hitherto' in the Sports Palace Goebbels was 'suddenly painting everything very black and justifying the need for the stringent measures now being introduced'. A large part of the restrictions announced, such as the closure of nightclubs and shops selling luxury goods, could have happened much earlier but did not because it would have contradicted the 'official calculated optimism'. Nordmann did not at any rate expect the measures to have any decisive impact on the course of the war.[40]

The housewife Agnes Pausen from Heide in Holstein wrote on 20 February 1943 to her husband fighting on the eastern front that the speech had been 'terribly serious'. She had 'felt a little panicky for the first time really', though there had been 'actually nothing new' in it; it had merely been about organizing 'work in a really sensible way again'.[41]

Iring Fetscher, then aged 21 and later a political scientist, was stationed as a soldier in the occupied Netherlands and had, according

to his own account, a somewhat distanced and critical attitude to
the National Socialist regime. The rally as a piece of theatre, however,
roused him to real enthusiasm, as he recorded on 19 February in his
diary: 'Brilliant public address springing from a unique and intense
national ecstasy. Ten questions put to the German nation with biblical
solemnity; it all has the feel of a vast, powerful drama whose depth,
tragic quality, and significance were probably barely understood by a
single person present.' Decades later Fetscher found it difficult to
understand the evident enthusiasm he felt then. In retrospect he tried
to offer this explanation: 'Perhaps it was the speaker's ostentatious
"candour" that stood out so strikingly from the euphemistic formula-
tions used in many reports of the Wehrmacht High Command, perhaps
also the fascination exerted by the language itself.' The matter at any
rate went on troubling Fetscher and his confusion about his response
back then prompted his book project on the speech.[42]

To sum up, official reports as well as private writings suggest that
among the population the speech was received in a variety of ways and
certainly did not produce the enormous 'jolt' that might have made a
critical difference to everyday life in wartime Germany. By many it
was seen as a piece of propaganda that, while perfectly staged, was for
that very reason all too transparent, not least as far as its climax, the ten
questions, was concerned. It gave rise on the one hand to anxiety and
on the other to questions and criticism concerning things neglected in
the past, as well as to fears about a drift towards class conflict, in other
words towards developments that would split the 'national community'.
There were those who noted the failure to announce further substantial
measures to reshape the 'home front' and expressed doubts about the
just distribution of increased war burdens. Above all, Goebbels had
clearly not succeeded in communicating his crucial concern, namely
to convince people that his speech was the authentic expression of a
desire deeply rooted in the nation to embrace total war.

The sceptical and contradictory reactions described above can in
the final analysis be explained by the design of the whole enterprise.
Goebbels had made an emotionally charged speech to the committed
core of Berlin National Socialists, making use of 'arguments' and rhetorical means precisely tailored to this audience, in a space familiar to
them as an old 'battleground'. Such an event for insiders could never
have the same impact on the average audience in Germany as a whole

as in this hall itself, and the more Goebbels ramped up his rhetoric the more blatant became his propagandistic purpose.

As far as the impact of the speech is concerned, Goebbels appears not to have been quite sure whether Hitler would express publicly the strong approval of his initiative that he had conveyed to Goebbels afterwards. When, on the occasion of the celebration of the founding of the Party in Munich on 24 February, Hitler had a proclamation read out (his aversion to appearing in public continued), Goebbels, who had remained in Berlin ('I'm pretending to have the flu'[43]), was pleased and relieved to note that Hitler's declaration 'was fully consonant with my Sports Palace speech'. 'So there's no danger of my being in any way disavowed here.... It's evident again in this instance that it's best to create *faits accomplis*. If the nation accepts these then the battle's won.'[44]

A few days later, however, Goebbels learnt from Ley that in Munich there had in fact been 'grumbling from various quarters about my Sports Palace speech, and indeed the reasons are entirely transparent. The people who before the takeover of power were pleased if a leading Party comrade had a success as a speaker are now eaten up with envy. They hate to see other people working because it shows up their own complacency.'[45] Most probably it was not purely envy, however, that caused leading Party comrades to grumble about the speech. More likely they felt provoked and annoyed that Goebbels was evidently using his performance to attempt to incite a palace revolution designed to strengthen his own position.

'Total war' and the persecution of the Jews

As I have already mentioned in my commentary on the speech, the anti-Semitic elements served the important purpose of preparing National Socialists in the capital for the arrest and deportation of the Berlin Jews. On 27 February the so-called factory operation, the arrest by the SS-Leibstandarte (Hitler's bodyguard) of more than 8,000 Jews still working in the armaments industry, did in fact begin in the city. The majority were arrested at their workplaces.[46]

At the beginning of March deportations to Auschwitz were already getting under way. As Goebbels noted in his diary, 'here too' it has 'again emerged that the more elevated social classes, in particular intellectuals, don't understand our Jewish policy and to some extent take the side of the Jews. As a result our operation was leaked and consequently a lot of Jews have slipped through the net.'[47] According to his sources a total of around 4,000 people had escaped.[48] He would not, however, 'rest until at least the capital' was 'completely free of Jews'.[49]

While this was going on, during the night of 1 to 2 March Berlin experienced its heaviest air raid to date, resulting in a temporary state of emergency in the city. In view of the turbulence, Goebbels opposed the Security Service's plan to proceed with the deportations in spite of their being very controversial, especially as 'rather unpleasant scenes' had 'taken place outside a Jewish old people's home': 'people formed quite a big crowd and some even spoke up for the Jews'. He was therefore instructing the Security Service personnel responsible 'to cease evacuating the Jews at such a critical moment. We are happy to put it off for a few weeks more; then we can get it done all the more thoroughly.'[50] Three days later Hitler was to give him his full support over this.[51] In giving 'instructions' to the Security Service Goebbels was, however, exceeding his powers and in fact the deportations continued.

On 11 March Goebbels wrote in his diary: 'Unfortunately, to begin with Jews and Jewesses in privileged marriages were arrested at the same time, producing immense fear and confusion.' He was alluding to protests primarily from people in 'mixed marriages' with Jews who had been arrested in the operation. The fact that some 2,000 such Jews, who were temporarily held in the building housing the Jewish community administration in Rosenstrasse, were released a few days later was, however, most probably not the result of Goebbels's intervention nor of protests from the relatives. Rather, the Security Service had never intended to deport this group of people.[52]

In a telephone conversation on 14 March Hitler supported Goebbels's intention 'to get the Jews out of the entire territory of the Reich as quickly as possible'. In addition, he instructed him 'to give greater emphasis again to the Jewish question in our propaganda; for after all it's the Jews who are pushing England towards gradual bolshevization'.[53]

A few days later Hitler appeared to him to be 'extraordinarily concerned' by the fact that even after the most recent deportations 17,000 Jews still lived in so-called mixed marriages in Berlin. As Goebbels learnt, Hitler gave 'Frick the task of making it easier to dissolve such marriages and to pronounce them dissolved if no more than a wish to divorce is expressed'. Goebbels gave complete support to this move.[54] At the ministerial briefing on 1 April he ordered the number of vacated 'Jewish dwellings' to be made known by word of mouth, in order to alert the population to the advantages to be gained from the deportations.[55] He was convinced furthermore 'that freeing Berlin of Jews is one of my greatest political achievements'.[56]

Intrigues, power games, and illusions: 'total war' never happens

Spurred on by the supposed enormous impact of his 'total war' speech and in response to efforts by others to limit his influence on the Committee of Three, Goebbels developed an alternative to his original plan of gaining the central role he coveted in domestic policy via this committee. With Speer, Ley, and Funk as allies, in March he attempted 'to neutralize the so-called Committee of Three by reviving the Ministerial Council for the Defence of the Reich'. This council, created at the outbreak of war as a kind of war cabinet, had, however, failed to live up to this ambitious aspiration. Instead it had developed into an instrument for simplifying legislation by issuing Ministerial Council decrees via a circulation process—without holding any meetings at all. The intended reanimation was to consist in giving Göring, the chairman of the non-convening Council, who was increasingly lapsing into passivity, a dynamic deputy in the person of Goebbels. According to his diary, Goebbels then intended with the help of around ten men (all of them 'capital fellows') to 'govern, in other words to set up a domestic political leadership'.[57] Göring received Goebbels in early March in Berchtesgaden and agreed to the plan to 'transfer the executive functions of the Reich from the Committee of Three to the Ministerial Council for the Defence of the Reich'. The names Himmler, Ley, Speer, and Funk came up as possible new members of the Ministerial Council.[58]

On his next visit to the Führer's Headquarters in Vinnitsa on 8 March, however, Goebbels unfortunately discovered that 'Göring's prestige with the Führer' had 'plummeted', and in fact Hitler told him confidentially that he wanted to stand Göring down.[59] Even so, Goebbels and his associates did not give up their plan but simply waited for a favourable opportunity to propose it to Hitler. On 17 March Goebbels, Speer, Ley,

and Funk met again, this time with Göring too, and established further
details as a way of setting up 'clear leadership in domestic policy', not
least with the aim of ousting Bormann and Lammers, both members
of the Committee of Three, from their central position in domestic
policy and limiting Keitel, the third member, to his military role.[60]

In parallel with his efforts, bordering on a conspiracy, to get rid of
the Committee of Three, Goebbels continued to take part in its meetings. In February and March it concerned itself with, among other
things, such trivial topics as the standardization of wage deductions
and the simplification of tax laws, with university cuts, various bits of
administrative rationalization, and restrictions on the appointment and
promotion of civil servants.[61] That was certainly not the kind of 'leadership in domestic politics' that Goebbels was aiming for.

Patently frustrated by the Committee's mode of operating, Goebbels
made his mark at the meetings by driving things forward and stirring
things up. On 27 February he demanded that the Wehrmacht adopt
'more vigorous measures' to achieve the planned call-up targets, and
when Keitel intervened he complained that Keitel's offices were 'in
need of reform'. Then on 16 March, when university cuts were being
discussed, he asserted 'that the daughters of posh families go to university
in order to dodge war work'. At the same meeting, when a decree to
counter the sabotaging of 'total' war was under discussion, he demanded
that the death penalty be introduced for serious cases.[62]

In a string of instances, however, it can be shown that in his diary
Goebbels overstated his role in the meetings and presented an exaggerated account of the 'successes' he achieved, presumably overestimating
their importance. At any rate, in spite of his being a powerful advocate
of radical action, many measures he pressed for or even considered
already settled simply did not happen or only in a reduced form.

Thus, for example, on 16 March he considered the 'reform of the
justice system' to have been implemented 'now entirely in line with
my ideas'; in particular, appeals in civil trials would in future be discontinued. The minutes indicate, however, that in fact nothing more than
a simplification of the appeals process was agreed.[63] In his diary Goebbels
wrote that in the same meeting he severely criticized the way conscription to the armed forces was conducted, yet his contribution was
completely omitted from the minutes after Keitel asked for the item to
be taken off the agenda. He likewise congratulated himself on having
succeeded in shutting down the Reich Central Office for Land Use,

though there was only a decision to restrict the scope of its work.[64] Having had horse riding banned in the Berlin Tiergarten park, Goebbels involved Hitler in an attempt to ban racing of any kind. In this he failed because Hitler decided that it should instead continue on a reduced scale, arguing that, among other things, 'entertainment for the general public' must be 'safeguarded, even in wartime'.[65]

Goebbels's proposals for total war not only met with growing resistance in the Committee of Three, but, having vaunted himself so vigorously in public as the tribune of 'total war', he was now in danger of being blamed for its half-hearted implementation. From the Security Service reports he was aware on the one hand of approval of the planned measures for 'total war', but on the other of growing criticism that the steps taken had not been radical enough. As he states in his diary, 'no storm has broken forth yet…as I announced it would in my Sports Palace speech'.[66]

When in early March Goebbels read complaints in the Security Service report that 'hints of class conflict had found their way into the propaganda for total war' and that these had had a negative effect on sections of the population,[67] he immediately responded. It was simply inevitable, he declared in an article in Das Reich, that 'total war' involved a 'certain levelling'; this resulted, however, not 'from envy or class consciousness' but from 'overwhelming necessity linked to a specific purpose'.[68] In a further article in the following edition of Das Reich he returned to the theme, indignant that 'a few hotheads, for example, are trying to exploit a good opportunity to let off steam about their half-baked sense of class'.[69]

It is evident that Goebbels, who had so often relished his role as advocate of a 'socialist direction' in the NSDAP and as recently as the previous November had expatiated in Das Reich about the 'War as a Social Revolution', feared that he might fall under the not entirely groundless suspicion of wishing to introduce a sort of wartime communism.

The 'slow re-emergence of spring and summer illusions' in the population in the course of spring 1943 forced Goebbels to recognize that doubt was increasingly being cast by all sorts of official bodies on his ideas of how to implement 'total war'.[70] In addition, Hitler himself was only too ready to react positively to such counter-initiatives. As Goebbels noted, these included such disparate things as the reappearance of popular magazines, the reopening of casinos, inconsistencies in the implementation of women's obligation to work, the lifting of restrictions on leisure travel, and other such developments.[71] All of a piece with this was the fact that, to Goebbels's great disappointment, Hitler was not prepared to call to account leading members of the political class (amongst them Interior Minister Frick, Foreign Minister Ribbentrop, and Agriculture Minister Walther Darré) who had bene-fited from the illicit sales of gourmet food by the Berlin delicatessen owner August Nöthling, exposed in early 1943.[72]

Although he continued to pursue the idea of gaining Göring's cooperation in his plans for 'total war', shortly before a crucial meeting on 12 April in Berchtesgaden Goebbels suffered 'a terrible attack of kidney trouble'. With Göring as chair and with powerful support from Goebbels, the meeting was to discuss the reorganization of labour with the aim of mobilizing more German workers instead of making use of increasing numbers of foreign slave workers. Without his focus and specialist knowledge, as he recorded in his diary, the plan to use the meeting to inaugurate a new political phase was doomed to failure.[73] Having discussed the situation again in early May with Speer and also with Funk and Ley, he no longer believed 'that at the moment it's possible to persuade Göring to take over leadership of domestic affairs', as he is 'somewhat battered'.[74]

Although Goebbels continued to profess himself convinced that Hitler supported 'unreservedly' the principle of 'total war'[75] (a belief even Speer encouraged him in),[76] the reality looked rather different. On 9 May, for example, Hitler announced to him categorically that 'in total war' there must be 'no war against women..., as soon as their beauty treatments are affected we'll have made them our enemies'. Casinos and horseracing were necessary, he said, to absorb purchasing power.[77] Goebbels and his associates had planned a comprehensive 'reform of the Reich' for the period after the war and hoped to be able already 'to implement it to a modest extent by stealth through the measures for total war'.[78] A few days later Goebbels learned that Hitler strongly opposed this.

In spite of everything, Goebbels regarded himself as committed: 'The nation associates the thinking and ideas of total war with me personally. I am therefore in a certain sense publicly responsible for the continued pursuit of total war.'[79]

His solution to this dilemma consisted in making the theme of 'total war' less prominent in the ensuing months and in finding outlets in other political areas for his radicalism. The discovery of the mass graves of Polish officers shot by the Soviet secret police, for example, provided an opportunity to exploit it as part of a large-scale anti-Semitic propaganda campaign. As the year progressed there were different challenges; at least a year went by after he had temporarily given up his efforts to bring about 'total war' before he had the chance again to revive his plans to introduce it. This time he would get his way with Hitler.

From 'total war' to total defeat

In the summer of 1944, eighteen months after the Sports Palace speech, Goebbels made a further attempt to make his mark as the radical advocate of 'total war' and to acquire a central leadership role on the German 'home front' above and beyond his function as propaganda chief.

After the winter crisis of 1941/2 and the catastrophe of Stalingrad the previous year the 'Third Reich' was facing a new and serious military challenge: After landing in Normandy on 6 June, Allied troops had created a bridgehead that was being reinforced continuously almost without hindrance with further troops and matériel; meanwhile, in its summer offensive launched on 22 June the Red Army was exploiting the concentration of German forces on the western front to destroy Army Group Centre and open up a wide gap in the German front line on the eastern front. In addition, on 4 June the Wehrmacht had been forced to withdraw from Rome and in July, as a result of systematic enemy bombing, the production of synthetic fuel crucial to supplying the Wehrmacht broke down so dramatically that, among other things, aviation fuel became scarce.

Goebbels at first tried yet again to use a personal discussion with Hitler on 21 June on the Obersalzberg to convince him of the need to introduce total war, but Hitler rejected the plan.[80] He immediately tried to get his ideas accepted in spite of this by again seeking an alliance with Speer. Both ministers wrote memoranda to Hitler.

Speer[81] concentrated on setting out the familiar demands for a further intensification of the war effort (above all the closure of businesses, increase in female labour, and reduction of administrative staff), supporting his argument with figures. Goebbels's memorandum[82] of 18 July 1944 was principally concerned with demonstrating to Hitler that the nation's will and strength had to be exerted to their utmost if 'total war' were truly to be waged with a resulting change of fortune on the battlefield.

In the process he turned again to central themes in his Sports Palace speech: The necessity of fundamentally overhauling the bureaucracies of the Wehrmacht and civil administration, as well as civilian life, in order finally to achieve the so urgently needed 'true state of war'. In an almost peremptory tone he made a detailed proposal for the implementation of these tasks: 'My Führer, for each task that has to be undertaken—and these can easily be established in a meeting with you—give the most wide-ranging authority to a man in whom you have confidence. Commission him to develop a plan of action for you very soon. Give one of these men the task of coordinating these plans and then presenting them to you along with all those involved. Then each of them, vested with your complete confidence, shall get to work.' The primary requirements of these individuals were to be 'imagination, political passion, profound belief', characteristics in other words that by his own judgement he, Joseph Goebbels, had in abundance. The fact too that the memorandum was strewn with reminiscences of the 'time of struggle' they had gone through together and of crises the regime had survived could only be read as blatant self-promotion. These measures he was proposing, Goebbels promised, would give 'an incredible boost to the mood of the entire nation'.

Fundamentally he was therefore taking the same voluntaristic approach as he had the previous year: His concept of 'total war' was not technocratic, as Speer's was, but rather rooted in ethno-nationalist ideology. In the end, however, Speer came to the same conclusion in his memorandum as Goebbels and called for 'a new figure, equipped with all necessary powers' as a way of solving the crisis; according to his memoirs he had already named Goebbels as a suitable candidate.[83] This coordinated internal initiative on the part of the two men was accompanied by a renewed public campaign (admittedly limited compared with that of the previous year), which Goebbels launched in early July with a leading article in *Das Reich* provocatively entitled 'Are we waging total war?' and a 'rousing' speech in Breslau (Wrocław).

Two days after Goebbels had finished his memorandum, there was an attempt on Hitler's life at his headquarters at the Wolf's Lair. In this situation no one in the top leadership could continue to resist serious and more radical efforts to win the war—and this circumstance played into Goebbels's hands. On 22 July at a meeting with Lammers he found that not only the head of the Reich Chancellery and his ally Speer but also Keitel and Bormann had in the meantime accepted the idea of a more radical approach to the war. As Lammers put it, they all agreed to task Goebbels with a comprehensive 'reform of our public life'.[84]

Even so, Goebbels, in spite of his efforts, was not in the end to be put in charge of the 'overall coordination' of measures to promote 'total war' but merely of certain sectors. Hitler had already appointed Himmler commander of the relief army on 20 July and given him special powers in military affairs. The same day he had also given Bormann responsibility for implementing 'total war' within the Nazi Party.[85] Speer's control over armaments was in any case unaffected.

On 23 July the results of the previous day's meeting were confirmed at a conference chaired by Hitler. The only person within the leadership still creating difficulties was Göring, who had not attended the meeting on 22 July. He felt passed over and declared peevishly that he 'was practically forced to resign'.[86] As a result, the 'Führer Decree concerning Total War'[87] issued two days later was worded in such a way as to include Göring, who was given the prerogative to make the first proposal for the appointment of the 'Reich Plenipotentiary'. Since, however, it had already been decided that Goebbels was to be given the job, this was a purely formal measure that once again served no other purpose than to avoid damaging Göring's prestige.

This somewhat cumbersome procedure was in itself a sign that as the prospective 'Reich Plenipotentiary for Total War' Goebbels by no means enjoyed the comprehensive powers promised in his title. If, in spite of this, he claimed that 'a domestic war dictatorship' had effectively been set up and boasted that he had 'received the greatest powers hitherto granted in the National Socialist Reich' and achieved 'probably the greatest success of [his] life'[88] then he was turning a blind eye—as he so often did in matters concerning his personal success story—to a number of significant and, for him, disagreeable aspects.

While the decree provided for the Reich Plenipotentiary to have a general right to direct the supreme Reich authorities, it simultaneously already outlined an appeals procedure. The power to issue 'legal provisions and basic administrative instructions' in the field of 'total war' remained with the individual supreme Reich authorities, and with regard to military matters, the Party, and armaments Goebbels was given no powers. A few days later Lammers produced a further document that listed those central departments in addition to his own Chancellery that were not subject to directives from the Reich Plenipotentiary.[89]

Regardless of this, Goebbels immediately threw himself into his new tasks. On 3 August he made a speech to Gauleiters meeting in Posen (Poznań) and afterwards claimed in his diary that he was confident of their active cooperation.[90] The Gauleiters did in fact chair the newly created 'Gau commissions' in which representatives of various authorities and Party functionaries were supposed to work together to identify potential Wehrmacht recruits in the relevant administrations. This process was to reach down even to local district level.[91] This move was motivated only in part by a wish to deploy people more effectively for the purposes of 'total war' for representatives of the Party now also saw an opportunity of finally gaining the upper hand in the power struggle they had been engaged in since 1933 with the state and its institutions. Opponents, on the other hand, resisted forcefully what they saw as an all too obvious attempt to hobble the state bureaucracy.[92]

Also in August Goebbels sent a circular to the supreme Reich authorities warning them that in future administrative offices should work 'until the tasks in hand are completed' but for a minimum of sixty hours per week. In a further circular he also instructed the authorities to move to a 'war footing' and in future do without receptions, inauguration ceremonies, memorial events, and the like.[93]

As he had intended back in 1943, Goebbels now raised the upper age limit for compulsory work for women from forty-five years to fifty.[94] Although Hitler consented to his raising it again to fifty-five years this measure was never implemented.[95] In addition, Goebbels put his principal effort into using closures and rationalizations to move labour out of administrative offices and non-essential industries and services. Thus, for example, postal deliveries were reduced, ticket inspection on the railways simplified, various publications shut down, vocational colleges closed, the 'burden of form-filling' allegedly removed, and all congresses and conferences cancelled. Goebbels kept Hitler up to date with all these measures in so-called Führer bulletins.[96]

It was not long, however, before the Reich Plenipotentiary was forced to admit that he was unable to implement a number of the measures he had so boldly decreed because he did not have the necessary powers to intervene in the activities of other ministries. On top of this, he quickly became aware of strong defenders of the status quo everywhere. Though only half-willing to admit it to himself, Goebbels knew that their staunchest support came from Hitler himself, who, as in the previous year, feared that too much 'total war' might lead to general chaos and a further slump in the public mood.

In spite of this, in August Goebbels pressed on with closing down theatres, orchestras, and music halls in the face of Hitler's 'very strong resistance',[97] though for months afterwards he was forced to cope with appeals against closure and attempts to reopen.[98] Hitler, on the other hand, blocked Goebbels's plan to stop people sending parcels and private telegrams.[99] He also opposed the halting of production of beer and confectionary.[100] Although in August he began by approving Goebbels's wish to suspend publication of art journals, he was persuaded by the objection of an interested party to postpone this measure until 1 January 1945.[101]

Lammers and Bormann successfully intervened with Hitler to thwart Goebbels's attempt to abolish the office of Minister President of Prussia, which Göring was holding on to with an iron grip. They were also able to block his plan to abolish the Reich Economics Ministry and other supreme Reich authorities.[102] This strongly suggests that Hitler was opposed to the reform of the Reich administration demanded by many experts as part of 'total war'.[103]

Goebbels established monthly quotas of Wehrmacht recruits to be removed from the administration, service industries, and armaments production (300,000 men for August, for example) and, as a complementary measure, worked to organize substitute labour for industries crucial to the war effort, primarily in the form of older women and redundant administrative staff.[104] These plans could be only partially realized, however, and were even counterproductive. It had been Goebbels's intention to supply the Wehrmacht with a total of 700,000 men in the months from August to October, but by the end of the year a total of only some 500,000 had been reached.[105] For its part the Wehrmacht could not keep up with the training of recruits, with the result that many highly skilled workers who had been released from their jobs were waiting around without any occupation,[106] while the labour exchanges could find work for only a fraction of those who signed on. Thus people often ended up unemployed.[107]

The 'unbureaucratic' way of working that Goebbels was aiming for led, among other things, to there being little paperwork by means of which to trace or evaluate his own projects and their efficiency. At best this can be done in a fragmentary and indirect way, for example on the basis of his diaries. These convey above all a clear impression of the Reich Plenipotentiary's erratic way of working, throwing himself into more and more new tasks and attempting to put his ministerial colleagues under huge pressure. He then held them responsible if success did not follow, while always giving himself credit for anything he could present as a positive achievement. And he was constantly moving on to a new task, attacking it with equal amounts of enthusiasm and doubtful efficiency.

In the final analysis, Goebbels was not even concerned about achievements measurable in statistics. Rather, his tireless activity aimed above all to make a crucial improvement in the 'visual appearance of the war', in other words to gear the public image of the 'Third Reich' completely to war and to allow as little scope as possible for disruptive discussions of the actual state of the war, let alone of the looming defeat. At the same time, his powers did offer him numerous opportunities to intervene in the internal organization of the ministries of his esteemed colleagues and to close down propaganda activities that were in competition with his ministry.[108]

In December 1944 Hitler extended Goebbels's powers to the Wehrmacht also. Now, with the help of the Gauleiters and their staff, he could review all the Wehrmacht administrative offices in order to release soldiers for the front. In January 1945 alone the Wehrmacht recorded losses of 450,000 and in each of the remaining months of the war around 300,000 soldiers would be killed; to these were added many who were captured or whose serious injuries excluded them from further service.[109] The scale of these losses meant that in spite of all his efforts Goebbels was bound to lose his race against death on the battlefields of the Second World War. The upshot was that he made a significant contribution to the fact that hundreds of thousands of only superficially trained and inadequately armed German men were sent to the fronts as they were increasingly pushed back in the final phase of the war. A high percentage of these men died, while vast tracts of their own country were being destroyed beyond recognition.[110]

The de facto end of Goebbels's 'total war' was total defeat.

Acknowledgements

I should like to thank all the staff at the archives and libraries I used and everyone who helped to turn my manuscript into a book: my editor Ludger Ikas, my copy-editor Verena Simon, and also Tobias Angermann, Jens Dehning, and Arno Matschiner of the Siedler publishing house. I am grateful to Christian Schröder (Berlin) for alerting me to a photo providing evidence that Eugen Klöpfer and Bernhard Minetti were present at Goebbels's speech.

List of archives used

Bayerisches Hauptstaatsarchiv
BAB Bundesarchiv, Abt. Berlin
  R 43 II   Neue Reichskanzlei
BAK Bundesarchiv, Abt. Koblenz
  NL 1118   Nachlass Goebbels
  ZSg 102   Sammlung Sänger zur Pressepolitik des NS-Staats
  ZSg 109   Sammlung Oberweitmann zur Pressepolitik des NS-Staats
BAM Bundesarchiv, Abt. Militärarchiv Freiburg
  RH 15   OKH/Allgemeines Heeresamt (AHA)

Osoby Archive Moscow/Special Archive Moscow
  Fonds 1363–3 Reichsministerium für Volksaufklärung und Propaganda
  (Goebbels's ministerial briefings)

Notes

The abbreviation 'Goebbels TB' is used to refer to entries in Goebbels's diaries. See Elke Fröhlich (ed.), *Die Tagebücher von Joseph Goebbels*, 32 vols (Munich, 1993–2008).

INTRODUCTION

1. Sven Felix Kellerhoff, 'Wie Goebbels seine diabolische Rede inszenierte', in *Die Welt*, 18 February 2013 (https://www.welt.de/geschichte/zweiter-weltkrieg/article113703756/Wie-Goebbels-seine-diabolische-Rede-inszenierte.html); Rafael Seligmann, *Hitler. Die Deutschen und ihr Führer* (Berlin, 2004), 273 and 275.
2. For example in Hans Otto Regenhardt (ed.), *Forum Geschichte 9/10: Vom Kaiserreich bis zur Gegenwart* (Berlin, 2010), 187; or Michael Sauer (ed.), *Geschichte und Geschehen* (Stuttgart/Leipzig, 2013), 224.
3. Erich Ludendorff, *Der totale Krieg* (Munich, 2006); Johann Wilhelm Ludowici, *Totale Landesverteidigung* (Oldenburg/Berlin, 1936); 'Krieg', in Hermann Franke (ed.), *Handbuch der neuzeitlichen Wehrwissenschaften*, vol. 1 (Berlin/Leipzig, 1936); Guido Fischer, *Wehrwirtschaft. Ihre Grundlagen und Theorien* (Munich, 1936); Ernst Jünger's essay 'Die totale Mobilmachung', in Jünger, *Krieg und Krieger* (Berlin, 1931), 11–30; and Ernst Forsthoff, *Der totale Staat* (Hamburg, 1933) were all important in shaping Ludendorff's use of the term. On its history see also Gerhard Förster, *Totaler Krieg und Blitzkrieg. Die Theorie des totalen Krieges und des Blitzkrieges in der Militärdoktrin des faschistischen Deutschlands am Vorabend des 2. Weltkrieges* (Berlin, 1967); also Ludolf Herbst, *Der Totale Krieg und die Ordnung der Wirtschaft. Die Kriegswirtschaft im Spannungsfeld von Politik, Ideologie und Propaganda 1939–1945* (Stuttgart, 1982), 35ff.
4. Friedrich von Bernhardi, *Vom Krieg der Zukunft* (Berlin, 1920); Kurt Hesse, *Der Feldherr Psychologos. Ein Suchen nach den Führern der deutschen Zukunft* (Berlin, 1922); Hans Ritter, *Der Zukunftskrieg und seine Waffen* (Leipzig, 1924); George Soldan, *Der Mensch in der Schlacht der Zukunft* (Oldenburg, 1925); Jünger, 'Die totale Mobilmachung'.
5. Ludendorff, *Der totale Krieg*, 48.
6. Ibid., in particular 11ff.

7. For literature on the Sports Palace speech see Willi A. Boelcke, 'Goebbels und die Kundgebung im Berliner Sportpalast vom 18. Februar 1943', in *Jahrbuch für die Geschichte Mittel- und Ostdeutschlands*, 19 (1970), 234–55; Iring Fetscher, *Joseph Goebbels im Berliner Sportpalast 1943: 'Wollt ihr den totalen Krieg?'* (Hamburg, 1998); Jens Kegel, *'Wollt Ihr den totalen Krieg?' Eine semiotische und linguistische Gesamtanalyse der Rede Goebbels' im Berliner Sportpalast am 18. Februar 1943* (Tübingen, 2006); Günter Moltmann, 'Goebbels' Rede zum totalen Krieg am 18. Februar 1943', in *Vierteljahreshefte für Zeitgeschichte*, 12 (1964), 13–43.

I BEFORE THE SPEECH

1. I base the following comments on Goebbels's personality, career, and relationship with Hitler on my Goebbels biography, *Goebbels* (Munich, 2010; published in English translation as *Goebbels. A Biography* (London, 2015)). On Goebbels the man see also Lutz Hachtmeister and Michael Kloft (eds), *Das Goebbels-Experiment—Propaganda und Politik* (Munich, 2005); Helmut Heiber, *Joseph Goebbels* (Berlin, 1965); Ralf Georg Reuth, *Goebbels* (Munich/Zurich, 1990); Toby Thacker, *Joseph Goebbels. Life and Death* (London, 2009).
2. Goebbels TB, 22 November 1930 (referring to the event on the previous day).
3. Goebbels TB, 31 January 1940.
4. For a detailed account of Goebbels's policies in the winter crisis see my *Goebbels*, 495ff.
5. See, for example, the article 'Wann oder Wie?' in the weekly *Das Reich* for 9 November 1941, which he considered a landmark statement.
6. Goebbels TB, 2 January 1942.
7. Olaf Gröhler, *Bombenkrieg gegen Deutschland* (Berlin, 1990), 36ff.
8. Goebbels TB, 9, 24, 25, 28, 30, and 31 July, also 12 August 1942; Osoby Archive, Moskow, 1363–3 (Ministerial Briefings), 7 July and 15 August 1942.
9. Goebbels TB, 20 August 1942. Quotations in the following two paragraphs are from the same source.
10. See Goebbels TB, 13 to 16 August 1942.
11. Goebbels TB, 18 August 1942.
12. Goebbels TB, 19 August 1942.
13. Bernd Wegner, 'Der Krieg gegen die Sowjetunion 1941/43', in Horst Boog et al. (eds), *Der globale Krieg. Die Ausweitung vom Weltkrieg und der Wechsel der Initiative 1941–1943* (Stuttgart, 1990), 976ff.
14. Goebbels TB, 15 September 1942.
15. Goebbels TB, 16 September 1942; Osoby Archive, 1363–3 (Ministerial Briefings), 16 September 1942; Press instructions: BAK, ZSg 109/37, printed in Willi A. Boelcke (ed.), *Wollt ihr den totalen Krieg? Die geheimen Goebbels-Konferenzen 1939–43* (Herrsching, 1989), 363, also BAK, ZSg 102/40, 16 September 1942 (Midday), 1. Watchword of the day.

16. Longerich, *Goebbels*, 490.
17. Osoby Archive, 1363–3 (Ministerial Briefings), 26 September 1942.
18. Goebbels TB, 27 September 1941, see also 1 October 1942.
19. Adolf Hitler, *Reden und Proklamationen 1932–1945. Kommentiert von einem deutschen Zeitgenossen*, ed. Max Domarus, 2 vols (Neustadt a. d. Aisch, 1963), 1913ff., in particular 1916.
20. Goebbels TB, 2 October 1942.
21. Goebbels TB, 8 October 1942, also 11, 15, 16, 23, and 25 October 1942.
22. Goebbels TB, 23 October 1942.
23. See his personal assessment in TB, 1 and 2 October 1942.
24. *Das Reich*, 18 October and 1 November 1942.
25. See Wegner, 'Der Krieg gegen die Sowjetunion 1941/43', 995ff.
26. Goebbels TB, entries from 21 October 1942 onwards; for quotation see 26 October 1942.
27. Reinhard Stumpf, 'Der Krieg im Mittelmeerraum 1942/43: Die Operationen in Nordafrika und im Mittelmeer', in Horst Boog et al. (eds), *Der Globale Krieg*, 671ff. and 688ff.
28. *Das Reich*, 8 November 1942, 'Vor die Probe gestellt'.
29. On the Allied landing see Stumpf, 'Der Krieg im Mittelmeerraum 1942/43', 710ff.
30. Hitler, *Reden und Proklamationen*, vol. 2, 1933ff.
31. Stumpf, 'Der Krieg im Mittelmeerraum 1942/43', 720ff.
32. Goebbels TB, 23 December 1942.
33. Wegner, 'Der Krieg gegen die Sowjetunion 1941/43', 997ff.
34. Verordnung über die Reichsverteidigungskommissare und die Vereinheitlichung der Wirtschaftsverwaltung vom 16. November 1942, *Reichsgesetzblatt* 1942 I 649ff.
35. Goebbels TB, 26 November 1942.
36. Goebbels TB, 27 November 1942.
37. Goebbels TB, 28 November 1942.
38. For details see my *'Davon haben wir nichts gewusst!' Die Deutschen und die Judenverfolgung 1933–1945* (Munich, 2006), 222ff.
39. In his New Year address in 1942 he spoke of *Vernichtung* (destruction). Then in his speech on 30 January 1942 he used the term *Ausrottung* (extermination), and repeated it in his declaration at the celebration to mark the founding of the Party on 24 February, in a speech at the Sports Palace on 30 September 1942, and in his address at the commemoration of the Munich putsch on 9 November 1942 (Hitler, *Reden und Proklamationen*, vol. 2, 1828f., 1844, 1920, 1937, and 1992).
40. Vertrauliche Informationen der Partei-Kanzlei, Folge 66, 9. Oktober 1942, printed in my edited volume *Die Ermordung der europäischen Juden. Eine umfassende Dokumentation des Holocaust 1941–1945* (Munich, 1989), 433f.
41. Walter Laqueur, *Was niemand wissen wollte* (Frankfurt am Main/Berlin/Vienna, 1981), 186.

42. Ibid., 209ff.
43. Goebbels TB, 5, 6, and 9 December 1943.
44. The minutes of the Ministerial Briefings from which I quote are in the Osoby Archive in Moscow, catalogued under the shelfmark 1363-3-26.
45. Ibid., 14 December 1942.
46. Goebbels TB, for example 27 November and 18 December 1942.
47. Goebbels TB, 11, 12, and 15 December 1942.
48. Goebbels TB, 22 and 23 December 1942.
49. Goebbels TB, 18 and 23 December 1942.
50. Goebbels TB, 23 December 1942.
51. *Das Reich*, 27 December 1942, 'Die Vollendeten'; Goebbels TB, 16 December 1942.
52. Goebbels TB, 29 December 1942.
53. Goebbels TB, 29 November und 18 December 1942.
54. Goebbels TB, 5 January 1943.
55. Goebbels TB, 3 January 1943; BAB, R 43 II/655; see Ludolf Herbst, *Der Totale Krieg und die Ordnung der Wirtschaft. Die Kriegswirtschaft im Spannungsfeld von Politik, Ideologie und Propaganda 1939–1945* (Stuttgart, 1982), 199ff.
56. Goebbels TB, 3 January 1943 (Göring), 5 January 1943 (General von Unruh, Lammers, Gauleiter Terboven).
57. Willi A. Boelcke (ed.), *Wollt ihr den totalen Krieg? Die geheimen Goebbels-Konferenzen 1939–43* (Herrsching, 1989), 4 to 6 January 1943.
58. Goebbels TB, 5, 7, and 8 January 1943.
59. Goebbels TB, 9 January 1943; BAB, R 43 II/655, Einladung und Protokoll; on the meeting and the measures that followed see Dieter Rebentisch, *Führerstaat und Verwaltung im Zweiten Weltkrieg. Verfassungsentwicklung und Verfassungspolitik, 1939–1945* (Stuttgart, 1989), 474ff.; Herbst, *Der Totale Krieg*, 199ff.; Bernhard A. Kroener, '"Menschenbewirtschaftung", Bevölkerungsverteilung und personelle Rüstung in der zweiten Kriegshälfte (1942–1944)', in Kroener et al. (eds), *Organisation und Mobilmachung des deutschen Machtbereichs. Zweiter Halbband: Kriegsverwaltung, Wirtschaft und personelle Ressourcen 1942–1944/45* (Stuttgart, 1999), 847ff.
60. Goebbels TB, 10 and also 13 January 1943 on discussions with Bormann and Speer. Goebbels's diaries during these days are full of further avowals of the need for 'total war'.
61. On the writing of this article see Goebbels TB, 3 January 1943. See also the earlier article 'Die Heimat im Kriege', *Das Reich*, 3 January 1943; and Goebbels, *Die Zeit ohne Beispiel* (Munich, 1941), 113–20, in which he had expressed mainly admiration for the home front.
62. Goebbels TB, 16 January 1943.
63. *Das Reich*, 24 January 1943; Goebbels TB, 13 January 1943.
64. Martin Moll (ed.), *'Führer-Erlasse' 1939–1945. Edition sämtlicher überlieferter, nicht im Reichsgesetzblatt abgedruckter, von Hitler während des Zweiten Weltkriegs schriftlich erteilter Direktiven aus den Bereichen Staat, Partei, Wirtschaft,*

Besatzungspolitik und Militärverwaltung (Stuttgart, 1997), Document 222. Men between the ages of 17 and 65 and women between 17 and 50 were to be required to register; for Goebbels's comments see TB, 15 January 1943.

65. Goebbels TB, 5 January 1943 after discussion with Lammers.

66. Goebbels TB, 16 January 1943, see also 17 January 1943.

67. Goebbels TB, 18 January 1943.

68. Goebbels TB, 21 January 1943.

69. Goebbels TB, 3, 4, 8, and 9 January 1943.

70. Goebbels TB, 13 January 1943.

71. Goebbels TB, 15 January 1943.

72. This news was, however, put in a somewhat roundabout way: German troops in the city 'had for weeks [!] been engaged in heroic resistance against an enemy attacking it from all sides' [!], *Die Berichte des Oberkommandos der Wehrmacht 1939–1945,* Vol. 4: *1. Januar 1943 bis 31. Dezember 1943* (Cologne, 2004), 20.

73. Goebbels TB, 17 January 1943. See also 20 and 24 January 1943 on the deterioration of the public mood.

74. Goebbels TB, 1 to 21 January 1943.

75. Goebbels TB, 24 January, and also 25 and 31 January 1943.

76. Goebbels TB, 17 January 1943.

77. Goebbels TB, 23 January 1943.

78. BAK, ZSg 109/Vertrauliche Informationen vom 23. Januar 1943.

79. Though in his diary Goebbels creates the impression that this decision was a joint one, the decision was very probably largely his, if one bears in mind Hitler's predominant attitude to the issue of working women.

80. Goebbels TB, 24 January 1943.

81. Goebbels TB, 25 January 1943.

82. Ibid.

83. Goebbels TB, 26 January 1940.

84. Goebbels TB, 2 und 5 February 1940.

85. Goebbels TB, 27 January 1943.

86. Goebbels TB, 29 January 1943, transcript in BAB, R 43 II/654a. At the meeting the decision was made on the final wording of the decree for the release of labour for tasks vital to the war effort (*Reichsgesetzblatt* 1943 I 75f.), which was to be implemented through three circulars of 30 January 1943 (R 43 II/662). The final report of the Committee of Three from summer 1944 put the number of those released by the closures at 150,000 (R 43 II/664a).

87. Goebbels TB, 28 January 1943.

88. 7 February 1943, also printed in Goebbels, *Der steile Aufstieg, Reden und Aufsätze aus den Jahren 1942/43* (Munich, 1943), 159–66. Similar views can be found in the article 'Der Blick nach vorne', which appeared on 31 January (also printed in *Der steile Aufstieg,* 151–8).

89. Goebbels TB, 19, 21, and 23 January 1943.

90. Goebbels TB, 30 January 1943 on the preparations.
91. *Deutsche Allgemeine Zeitung*, 27 January 1943, 'Churchill bei—Roosevelt'; *Frankfurter Zeitung*, 27 January 1943, 'Der Ruf nach "Koordination". Churchill trifft sich mit Roosevelt—Wer soll in Afrika befehlen?'
92. 'England läuft den USA nach, Dritter Besuch Churchills bei Roosevelt'.
93. Goebbels TB, 26 January 1943, also 27 January: According to these entries it was not known where the 'gangster bosses' had met. On the conference see Norbert F. Pötzl, *Casablanca 1943. Das geheime Treffen, der Film und die Wende des Krieges* (Munich, 2017).
94. *Völkischer Beobachter*, 28 January 1943.
95. Goebbels TB, 28 January 1943.
96. At the ministerial briefing of 27 January 1943, printed in Willi A. Boelcke (ed.), *Wollt ihr den totalen Krieg? Die geheimen Goebbels-Konferenzen 1939–43* (Herrsching, 1989).
97. For additional reports in leading papers see *Deutsche Allgemeine Zeitung*, 28 January 1943, 'Roosevelt tagte in Casablanca. Mit Churchill, Giraud und de Gaulle, aber ohne einen Vertreter Stalins'; 29 January 1943, 'Das Weiße Haus in der östlichen Hemisphäre' and 'Was England an Casablanca vermißt'; *Frankfurter Zeitung*, 28 January 1943, 'Das Zusammentreffen Churchills mit Roosevelt'; 29 January 1943, leading article: 'Was in Casablanca nicht erreicht worden ist'; *Völkischer Beobachter*, 1 February 1943, leading article: 'Nachtrag zu Casablanca'.
98. Ministerial briefing, 27 January 1943. Surprisingly, in the provincial Brandenburg papers the *Seelower Tageblatt* and the *Teltower Kreisblatt*, where the reporting is virtually identical, there is an almost casual reference to the demand for 'unconditional surrender' ('Der Bluff von Casablanca').
99. Goebbels TB, 28 January 1943.
100. *Völkischer Beobachter* (Nuremberg edn), 31 January 1943, 'The Führer's Proclamation on 30 January 1943: Germany's Response: Struggle and Victory!' (headline). The text of Goebbels's speech followed the next day: 'Reich Minister Dr Goebbels in the Sports Palace: "Fierce determination lifts our hearts"'. The quotations included here, however, are based on the original recording, as they are in Helmut Heiber (ed.), *Goebbels-Reden 1932–1945*, 2 vols (Düsseldorf, 1972), vol. 2. Extracts are also available at archive.org.
101. Goebbels TB, 31 January 1943.
102. Ibid.
103. Heinz Boberach (ed.), *Meldungen aus dem Reich 1938–1945. Die geheimen Lageberichte des Sicherheitsdienstes der SS*, 17 vols (Herrsching, 1984), vol. 12, 1 February 1943, 4732f.
104. Goebbels TB, 4 February 1943, also 5 February 1943.
105. Goebbels TB, 5 February 1943.
106. Goebbels TB, 31 January/1 February 1943.
107. Goebbels TB, 2 February 1943.

108. Goebbels TB, 3 February 1943.
109. Ibid.
110. Goebbels TB, 4 February 1943; ZSg 109/4.2.43,Tagesparole 1.
111. *Das Reich*, 14 February 1943, 'Unser Wille und Weg'; Goebbels TB, 4 February 1943.
112. Goebbels TB, 6 February 1943, also 7 February 1943.
113. For Sauckel's presentation see Dok. 1739-PS, printed in *International Military Tribunal. Der Prozess gegen die Hauptkriegsverbrecher vor dem Internationalen Militärgerichtshof, 14. Oktober 1945 bis 1. Oktober 1946*, 42 vols (Nuremberg, 1947–9), vol. 27, 584ff. Goebbels's diary entry for 6 February 1942 does not mention this difference in the substance of the presentation but rather criticizes it as 'boring' and not detailed enough with regard to Gauleiters' future responsibilities.
114. Goebbels TB, 6 February 1943.
115. Goebbels TB, 8 February 1943.
116. Goebbels TB, 11 February 1945. These comments were not, however, recorded in the minutes of the meeting (BAB, R 43II/654a).
117. Goebbels TB, 13 February 1943.
118. BAB, R 43 II/655, notes by Lammers on 6 March and 10 May 1943.
119. Goebbels TB, 12 February 1943.
120. Goebbels TB, 15 February 1943. The SD reports from 11 February confirm that Stalingrad had 'caused the whole nation to reflect deeply'; there was a demand for effective action and a 'candid and sober review of the fundamental principles of political life'. See Boberach (ed.), *Meldungen aus dem Reich*, vol. 12, 4783.
121. Goebbels TB, 15 February 1943, also 16 and 18 February 1943.
122. BAK, ZSg 109/41, Vertrauliche Information vom 18. Februar 1943, II. Erläuterungen zur Tagesparole.
123. BAK, ZSg 102/42, 18 February (M), 10.
124. Goebbels TB, 18 February 1943.
125. *Das Reich*, 28 February 1943, also printed in Goebbels, *Der steile Aufstieg*, 205–12.

2 GOEBBELS'S SPEECH ON 'TOTAL WAR':
TEXT AND COMMENTARY

1. On the history of the Sports Palace see the essays in Alfons Arenhövel (ed.), *Arena der Leidenschaften. Der Berliner Sportpalast und seine Veranstaltungen 1920–1973* (Berlin, 1990). The volume also contains a list of all the events there.
2. Christa Schreier, 'Der Sportpalast in seiner baulichen Entwicklung', in *Arena der Leidenschaften*, 16–38 (17).
3. Goebbels TB, 15 September 1930.
4. Goebbels TB, 26 September 1938.

5. Goebbels TB, 19 August 1941.
6. Albert Speer, *Erinnerungen* (Berlin, 1999), 269.
7. In the version released for publication this sentence was altered: 'Germany, at any rate, does not intend to give way to this threat but rather to oppose it in a timely manner and if necessary with the most radical measures.'
8. Hitler, *Reden und Proklamation, 1978; Judenverfolgung und jüdisches Leben unter den Bedingungen der nationalsozialistischen Gewaltherrschaft*, vol. 1: *Tondokumente und Rundfunksendungen 1930–1946*, collected and ed. Walter Roller (Potsdam, 1996), no. 136.
9. See Chapter 1, n. 40.
10. See my *Propagandisten im Krieg. Die Presseabteilung des Auswärtigen Amtes unter Ribbentrop* (Munich, 1987), 97ff.
11. *Das Reich*, 4 October 1942 ('Das neue Europa') and also 15 November 1942 ('Die neue Ordnung').
12. See my *Goebbels*, 530f.
13. Ibid., 553.
14. *Völkischer Beobachter* (Berliner Ausgabe), 20 April 1942, 'In Dankbarkeit und Treue'. On this see my *Goebbels*, 511f.

3 AFTER THE SPEECH

1. Goebbels TB, 19 February 1943.
2. Ibid.
3. Goebbels TB, 20 February 1943.
4. Goebbels TB, 21 and 22 February 1943.
5. Unless otherwise indicated, I am drawing here in particular on Iring Fetscher's work, for he devotes almost a third of his book *Joseph Goebbels im Berliner Sportpalast 1943* (Hamburg, 1998) to international press responses to the Sports Palace speech. As a result of his extensive research in several dozen newspapers he provides the reader with long quotations and/or literal translations from the original articles, extracts from which I quote in the following pages.
6. Fetscher, *Goebbels*, 180ff., particularly emphasizes the comments of 20 February 1943 by the *ABC* Berlin correspondent, which were completely in line with German propaganda.
7. *Joseph Goebbels im Berliner Sportpalast 1943*, 211ff.
8. Goebbels TB, 20 and 21 February 1943.
9. *Joseph Goebbels im Berliner Sportpalast 1943*, 161ff.
10. 'Rede Dr. Goebbels über die Kriegsanstrengungen Deutschlands', and 'Die Kundgebung im Sportpalast'.
11. Goebbels TB, 21 February 1943.
12. Neue Zürcher Zeitung, 19 February 1943, 'Die Kundgebung im Sportpalast'.
13. *Joseph Goebbels im Berliner Sportpalast 1943*, 187ff.
14. Ibid., 161ff.

15. *The Times*, Late London Edition, 'Goebbels's Gloom'.

16. 'Goebbels Asks Total Unity before Red "Invasion" Threat'.

17. 21 February 1943, section 4, page 3, Edwin L. James, 'Herr Goebbels Finds the Going Very Hard'.

18. 'Red Army Running Wild, Reich in Peril, Goebbels Warns.'

19. Section page 6 B: 'Playing At Peace'. The writer was basing his comments in particular on Goebbels's brusque rejection of a 'gentle appearance of peace', though he was in fact referring to the lifestyle of the privileged classes.

20. Fetscher mentions among others the *Basler Bund*, the *Manchester Guardian*, the *Daily Herald*, and the *Boston Daily Globe* (162, 211ff., 224, 226, and 238).

21. Goebbels TB, 20 February 1943.

22. The *Chicago Daily Tribune* published a short summary of the content on page 1 on 19 February, as did the *Los Angeles Times* in a single column on page 3, followed by a comment piece on 20 February.

23. Goebbels TB, 20 February 1943.

24. Goebbels TB, 21 and 24 February 1943.

25. Printed in *Meldungen aus dem Reich*, vol. 12, 4831ff.

26. Bayerisches Hauptstaatsarchiv, Staatskanzlei: Regierungspräsidentenberichte: Oberbayern, 10. März 1943 (Nr. 6671), Ober- und Mittelfranken, 8. März 1943 (Nr. 6679), Niederbayern und Oberpfalz, 10. März 1943 (Nr. 6674), Unterfranken, 10. März 1943 (Nr. 6681), Schwaben, 10. März 1943 (Nr. 6684).

27. Hans Schütz (ed.), *Bamberger Berichte über Stimmung und Haltung der Bevölkerung des Oberlandesgerichtsbezirks Bamberg während des 2. Weltkrieges* (Bamberg, 1983), 70.

28. Klaus Oldenhage, 'Die Pfalz und das Saarland während des Krieges (1940–1945). Aus den Lageberichten des Oberlandesgerichtspräsidenten und Generalstaatsanwaltes in Zweibrücken', in *Jahrbuch für westdeutsche Landesgeschichte*, Part I: 5 (1979), 303–56, Part II: 6 (1980), 343–98, quotation 368. Oldenhage (p. 307) also provides the opinion quoted here of the lawyer Karl Siegel.

29. Report from the director of the Ministry's Propaganda Department on the first impressions made by the speech based on the information received from the Reich Propaganda Offices, 19 February 1943, quoted from Marlis G. Steinert, *Hitlers Krieg und die Deutschen. Stimmung und Haltung der deutschen Bevölkerung im Zweiten Weltkrieg* (Düsseldorf/Vienna, 1970), 335.

30. From the Propaganda Ministry files, quoted by Steinert, *Hitlers Krieg*, 335f.

31. Heiner Grub (ed.), *Der Briefwechsel der Eltern Hermann und Lore Grub*, vol. 1 (Stuttgart/Tübingen, 2004), 319f.

32. Walter Kempowski, *Das Echolot. Ein kollektives Tagebuch. Januar und Februar 1943*, Vol. IV: *16. bis 28. Februar 1943* (Munich, 2016), 19 February 1943, 178.

33. Margarete Liebel to Christian Krause, 18 February 1943, in Joachim Krause (ed.), *Fremde Eltern. Zeitgeschichte in Tagebüchern und Briefen 1933–1945*, 2nd edn (Beucha, 2016).

34. Ibid., 281 and 283.

35. Friedrich Kellner, 'Vernebelt, verdunkelt sind alle Hirne'. Tagebücher 1939–1945, ed. Sascha Feuchert et al. (Göttingen, 2011), 19 February 1943.
36. Andreas-Friedrich, Der Schattenmann. Tagebuchaufzeichnungen 1938–1945 (Berlin, 1947), 107 (19 February 1943).
37. Matthias Joseph Mehs, Tagebücher. November 1929 bis September 1946, 2 vols, Vol. 2: Januar 1936 bis September 1946, ed. Günter Wein and Franziska Wein (Trier, 2011), 18 February 1943.
38. Victor Klemperer, Ich will Zeugnis ablegen bis zum letzten. Tagebücher 1933–1945, 2 vols, ed. Walter Nowojski, 7th edn (Berlin, 1997), vol. 2, 19 February 1943. In fact the wording of the threat in the printed version was that 'the most radical countermeasures' would be taken against the Jews.
39. Kempowski, Das Echolot, 19 February 1943, 175f.
40. Ibid., 19 February 1943, 181.
41. Ibid.
42. Fetscher, Goebbels, Foreword.
43. Goebbels TB, 23 February 1943.
44. Goebbels TB, 25 February 1943.
45. Goebbels TB, 27 February 1943.
46. Antonia Leugers (ed.), Berlin, Rosenstraße 2–4: Protest in der NS-Diktatur. Neue Forschungen zum Frauenprotest in der Rosenstraße 1943 (Annweiler, 2005); Wolf Gruner, Widerstand in der Rosenstraße. Die Fabrik-Aktion und die Verfolgung der 'Mischehen' 1943 (Frankfurt am Main, 2005).
47. Goebbels TB, 2 March 1943.
48. Goebbels TB, 11 March 1943.
49. Goebbels TB, 2 March 1943.
50. Goebbels TB, 6 March 1943.
51. Goebbels TB, 9 March 1943.
52. This argument is put forward convincingly by Gruner in Widerstand in der Rosenstraße, 85ff.
53. Goebbels TB, 15 March 1943; see also the entry for 20 March about a further conversation with Hitler about the deportations.
54. Goebbels TB, 18 April 1943.
55. Minutes of the Ministerial Briefing BAK, NL 1118/NL 138, 1 April 1943. He rejected the suggestion of stating the number of dwellings openly in propaganda, however.
56. Goebbels TB, 18 April 1943.
57. Goebbels TB, 27 February 1943.
58. Goebbels TB, 1 and 2 March 1943.
59. Goebbels TB, 9 March 1943.
60. Goebbels TB, 18 March 1942.
61. Goebbels TB, 11 and 28 February, also 17 March; BAB, R 43 II/654a, Minutes of the meetings on 10 February and 16 March 1943. On the committee's deliberations see Dieter Rebentisch, Führerstaat und Verwaltung im Zweiten Weltkrieg. Verfassungsentwicklung und Verfassungspolitik, 1939–1945 (Stuttgart, 1989), 481ff.

62. BAB, R 43 II/654a, minutes of the meeting on 16 March 1943; Goebbels TB, 17 March 1943. The decree gave rise to general unease in the ministries and in the end was not promulgated (for relevant correspondence see R 43II/658).

63. Goebbels TB, 17 March 1943; BAB, R 43 II/654a, minutes of the meeting on 17 March 1943; war measures decree of 12 May 1943, Reichsgesetzblatt 1943 I 290f.

64. Compare Goebbels TB, 17 March 1943 with the minutes of the meeting of 16 March 1943.

65. Goebbels TB, 23 February, 5, 9, and 22 March 1943 (quotation): BAB, R 43 II/658a Führervorlage Goebbels A II 218 v. 18. Februar 1943; the file also contains a minute by Lammers about Hitler's decision of 4 March as well as a letter of 24 March 1943 from Lammers to the responsible Reich ministers concerning horse racing; on this see Rebentisch, *Führerstaat*, 490ff.; BAB, R 43 II/654a, minutes of the meeting on 17 March 1943 at which Goebbels's submission on this matter was accepted.

66. Goebbels TB, 17 March, also 12, 13, 20, 21, and 27 March 1943.

67. Goebbels TB, 6 March 1943. In the SD report for 1 March 1943 it was stated that 'national comrades from the bourgeois classes felt put off by certain newspaper articles with what they described as a tone of "class struggle" '. It was difficult, the report said, to find suitable articles that took account of 'the sensitivity of national comrades not yet involved in war work and the scepticism and frequent self-righteousness of those classes already engaged in it.' See Boberach (ed.), *Meldungen aus dem Reich*, vol. 12, 4873.

68. *Das Reich*, 28 March 1943, 'Vom Unrecht im Kriege', also in Goebbels, *Der steile Aufstieg*, 228–36.

69. *Das Reich*, 4 April 1943, 'Ein offenes Wort zum totalen Krieg', also in Goebbels, *Der steile Aufstieg*, 237–42; Goebbels TB, 23 March and earlier on 6 March 1943.

70. Goebbels TB, 2 April 1943.

71. Goebbels TB, 2, 3, 6, and 29 April 1943.

72. Lothar Gruchmann, 'Korruption im Dritten Reich. Zur Lebensmittelversorgung der NS-Führerschaft', in *Vierteljahrshefte für Zeitgeschichte*, 42 (1994), 571–93. On this see also in particular Goebbels TB, 22 and 23 March, 7 and 19 May and also 23 July 1943.

73. Goebbels TB, 13 April 1943, also 14 to 19 April 1943 on his continuing complaints.

74. Goebbels TB, 6 and 7 May (quotation) 1943.

75. Goebbels TB, 7 May 1943, based on a meeting the previous day.

76. Goebbels TB, 6 May, also earlier on 24 April 1943.

77. Goebbels TB, 10 May 1943. See also the entry for 22 March 1943: 'Even the Führer takes the view that—just to take one example—we should not ban hair colouring for women.'

78. Goebbels TB, 20 May, also 11 May 1943.

79. Goebbels TB, 12 May 1943.
80. Goebbels TB, 22 June 1944.
81. Speer's memoranda of 12 and 20 July 1944, printed in Wolfgang Bleyer, 'Pläne der faschistischen Führung zum totalen Krieg im Sommer 1944', in Zeitschrift für Geschichtswissenschaft, 17 (1969), 1312–39.
82. See my 'Joseph Goebbels und der totale Krieg. Eine unbekannte Denkschrift des Propagandaministers vom 18. Juli 1944', in Vierteljahrshefte für Zeitgeschichte, 35 (1987), 289–314. Goebbels's close cooperation with Speer on this initiative emerges in particular from diary entries for July, which I discuss in detail in my Goebbels, 627f.
83. Speer, Erinnerungen, 405 (beginning of July).
84. BAB, R 43 II/664a, Protokoll der Chefbesprechung vom 22. Juli 1944; Goebbels TB, 23 July 1944; see my Goebbels, 631.
85. Decree of 20 July 1944 (Himmler), in Moll (ed.), Führer-Erlasse 1939–1945, no. 340; also the directive of 20 July 1944 (Bormann), ibid., no. 341.
86. Goebbels TB, 24 July 1944.
87. Reichsgesetzblatt 1944 I 161f.
88. Goebbels TB, 23 and 24 July 1944.
89. BAB, R 43 II/664a, 26 July 1944.
90. Goebbels TB, 4 August 1944.
91. Instruction of 16 August 1944, printed in Herbert Michaelis and Ernst Schraepler (eds), Ursachen und Folgen. Vom deutschen Zusammenbruch 1918 und 1945 bis zur staatlichen Neuordnung Deutschlands in der Gegenwart. Eine Urkunden- und Dokumentensammlung zur Zeitgeschichte, 27 vols (Berlin, 1958–79), vol. 21, no. 3528b.
92. Andreas Kunz, Wehrmacht und Niederlage. Die bewaffnete Macht in der Endphase der nationalsozialistischen Herrschaft, 1944 bis 1945 (Munich, 2005), 158.
93. BAB, R 43 II/666, 19. August 1944 also ibid., 665; this second circular, released with a date of 24 August, is printed in Michaelis and Schraepler (eds), Ursachen und Folgen, vol. 21, Nr. 666a.
94. Third decree concerning the registration of men and women for the defence of the Reich of 28 July 1944 (Reichsgesetzblatt, 1944 I 168).
95. Goebbels TB, 24 August 1944.
96. These measures are documented in Goebbels's 'Führer bulletins' and in press briefings issued by his ministry (collected in BAB, R 43 II/666b).
97. Goebbels TB, 24 August 1944.
98. Goebbels TB, 28 September and 4 November 1944.
99. BAB, R 43 II/665, letter from Bormann to Goebbels, 14 August 1944.
100. Goebbels TB, 24 August 1944.
101. Goebbels TB, 24 August and 5 October 1944.
102. See BAB, R 43 II/1363 for the relevant correspondence; Goebbels TB, 10 August 1944; Herbst, Der Totale Krieg, 344.
103. Goebbels TB, 24 October 1944.

104. Goebbels TB, 10 August 1944; for greater detail see my *Goebbels*, 639.
105. BAM, RH 15/126, Allgemeines Heeresamt, Stab II, Stand der Goebbels-Aktion vom 30. Dezember 1944, 1. Januar 1945; ibid. for a note of 23 January 1945 on the 'Luftwaffe quota'. For further details see my *Goebbels*, 640.
106. Goebbels TB, 7 October 1944 and 11 January 1945; Kunz, *Wehrmacht und Niederlage*, 180ff.
107. Goebbels TB, 17 September und 5 October 1944, 10 November 1944; BAB, R 43 II/666b, press communiqué, 2 November 1944; Kunz, *Wehrmacht und Niederlage*, 160.
108. For details see my *Goebbels*, 649.
109. Kunz, *Wehrmacht und Niederlage*, 155.
110. On the shortages of equipment and arms see ibid., 198ff.; there was not even an adequate supply of guns.

Bibliography

Andreas-Friedrich, Ruth, *Der Schattenmann. Tagebuchaufzeichnungen 1938–1945* (Berlin, 1947).

Arenhövel, Alfons (ed.), *Arena der Leidenschaften. Der Berliner Sportpalast und seine Veranstaltungen 1920–1973* (Berlin, 1990).

Bernhardi, Friedrich von, *Vom Krieg der Zukunft* (Berlin, 1920).

Bleyer, Wolfgang, 'Pläne der faschistischen Führung zum totalen Krieg im Sommer 1944', in *Zeitschrift für Geschichtswissenschaft*, 17 (1969), 1312–39.

Boberach, Heinz (ed.), *Meldungen aus dem Reich 1938–1945. Die geheimen Lageberichte des Sicherheitsdienstes der SS*, 17 vols (Herrsching, 1984).

Boelcke, Willi A., 'Goebbels und die Kundgebung im Berliner Sportpalast vom 18. Februar 1943', in *Jahrbuch für die Geschichte Mittel- und Ostdeutschlands*, 19 (1970), 234–55.

Boelcke, Willi A. (ed.), *Wollt ihr den totalen Krieg? Die geheimen Goebbels-Konferenzen 1939–43* (Herrsching, 1989).

Die Berichte des Oberkommandos der Wehrmacht 1939–1945, Vol. 4: *1. Januar 1943 bis 31. Dezember 1943* (Cologne, 2004).

Fetscher, Iring, *Joseph Goebbels im Berliner Sportpalast 1943: 'Wollt ihr den totalen Krieg?'* (Hamburg, 1998).

Fischer, Guido, *Wehrwirtschaft. Ihre Grundlagen und Theorien* (Munich, 1936).

Förster, Gerhard, *Totaler Krieg und Blitzkrieg. Die Theorie des totalen Krieges und des Blitzkrieges in der Militärdoktrin des faschistischen Deutschlands am Vorabend des 2. Weltkrieges* (Berlin, 1967).

Forsthoff, Ernst, *Der totale Staat* (Hamburg, 1933).

Franke, Hermann (ed.), *Handbuch der neuzeitlichen Wehrwissenschaften*, vol. I (Berlin/Leipzig 1936).

Fröhlich, Elke (ed.), *Die Tagebücher von Joseph Goebbels*, 32 vols (Munich, 1993–2008) (abbreviated in the notes to Goebbels TB).

Goebbels, Joseph, *Die Zeit ohne Beispiel* (Munich, 1941).

Goebbels, Joseph, *Der steile Aufstieg. Reden und Aufsätze aus den Jahren 1942/43* (Munich, 1943).

Gröhler, Olaf, *Bombenkrieg gegen Deutschland* (Berlin, 1990).

Grub, Heiner (ed.), *Der Briefwechsel der Eltern Hermann und Lore Grub*, vol. I (Stuttgart/Tübingen, 2004).

Gruchmann, Lothar, 'Korruption im Dritten Reich. Zur Lebensmittelversorgung der NS-Führerschaft', in *Vierteljahrshefte für Zeitgeschichte*, 42 (1994), 571–93.

Gruner, Wolf, *Widerstand in der Rosenstraße. Die Fabrik-Aktion und die Verfolgung der 'Mischehen' 1943* (Frankfurt am Main, 2005).

Hachmeister, Lutz and Michael Kloft (eds), *Das Goebbels-Experiment—Propaganda und Politik* (Munich, 2005).

Heiber, Helmut, *Joseph Goebbels* (Berlin, 1965).

Heiber, Helmut (ed.), *Goebbels-Reden 1932–1945*, 2 vols (Düsseldorf, 1972).

Herbst, Ludolf, *Der Totale Krieg und die Ordnung der Wirtschaft. Die Kriegswirtschaft im Spannungsfeld von Politik, Ideologie und Propaganda 1939–1945* (Stuttgart, 1982).

Hesse, Kurt, *Der Feldherr Psychologos. Ein Suchen nach den Führern der deutschen Zukunft* (Berlin, 1922).

Hitler, Adolf, *Reden und Proklamationen 1932–1945. Kommentiert von einem deutschen Zeitgenossen*, ed. Max Domarus, 2 vols (Neustadt a. d. Aisch, 1963).

International Military Tribunal. Der Prozess gegen die Hauptkriegsverbrecher vor dem Internationalen Militärgerichtshof, 14. Oktober 1945 bis 1. Oktober 1946, 42 vols (Nuremberg, 1947–9).

Judenverfolgung und jüdisches Leben unter den Bedingungen der nationalsozialistischen Gewaltherrschaft, Vol. 1: *Tondokumente und Rundfunksendungen 1930–1946*, collected and ed. Walter Roller (Potsdam, 1996).

Jünger, Ernst, 'Die totale Mobilmachung', in Jünger, *Krieg und Krieger* (Berlin, 1931), 11–30.

Kegel, Jens, *'Wollt Ihr den totalen Krieg?' Eine semiotische und linguistische Gesamtanalyse der Rede Goebbels' im Berliner Sportpalast am 18. Februar 1943* (Tübingen, 2006).

Kellner, Friedrich, *'Vernebelt, verdunkelt sind alle Hirne'. Tagebücher 1939–1945*, ed. Sascha Feuchert et al. (Göttingen, 2011).

Kempowski, Walter, *Das Echolot. Ein kollektives Tagebuch. Januar und Februar 1943, Vol. IV: 16. bis 28. Februar 1943* (Munich, 2016).

Klemperer, Victor, *Ich will Zeugnis ablegen bis zum letzten. Tagebücher 1933–1945*, 2 vols, ed. Walter Nowojski, 7th edn (Berlin, 1997).

Krause, Joachim (ed.), *Fremde Eltern. Zeitgeschichte in Tagebüchern und Briefen 1933–1945*, 2nd edn (Beucha, 2016).

Kroener, Bernhard R., '"Menschenbewirtschaftung", Bevölkerungsverteilung und personelle Rüstung in der zweiten Kriegshälfte (1942–1944)', in Kroener et al. (eds), *Organisation und Mobilmachung des deutschen Machtbereichs. Zweiter Halbband: Kriegsverwaltung, Wirtschaft und personelle Ressourcen 1942–1944/45* (Stuttgart, 1999) 777–1003.

Kunz, Andreas, *Wehrmacht und Niederlage. Die bewaffnete Macht in der Endphase der nationalsozialistischen Herrschaft, 1944 bis 1945* (Munich, 2005).

Laqueur, Walter, *Was niemand wissen wollte* (Frankfurt am Main/Berlin/Vienna 1981).

Leugers, Antonia (ed.), *Berlin, Rosenstraße 2–4: Protest in der NS-Diktatur. Neue Forschungen zum Frauenprotest in der Rosenstraße 1943* (Annweiler, 2005).

Lochner, Louis P. (ed.), *Goebbels Tagebücher aus den Jahren 1942–43* (Zurich, 1948).

Longerich, Peter, *Propagandisten im Krieg. Die Presseabteilung des Auswärtigen Amtes unter Ribbentrop* (Munich, 1987).

Longerich, Peter, 'Joseph Goebbels und der totale Krieg. Eine unbekannte Denkschrift des Propagandaministers vom 18. Juli 1944', in *Vierteljahrshefte für Zeitgeschichte*, 35 (1987), 289–314.

Longerich, Peter (ed.), *Die Ermordung der europäischen Juden. Eine umfassende Dokumentation des Holocaust 1941–1945* (Munich, 1989).

Longerich, Peter, *'Davon haben wir nichts gewusst!' Die Deutschen und die Judenverfolgung 1933–1945* (Munich, 2006).

Longerich, Peter, *Goebbels* (Munich, 2010).

Ludendorff, Erich, *Der totale Krieg* (Munich, 1935).

Ludowici, Johann Wilhelm, *Totale Landesverteidigung* (Oldenburg/Berlin, 1936).

Mehs, Matthias Joseph, *Tagebücher. November 1929 bis September 1946*, 2 vols, Vol. 2: *Januar 1936 bis September 1946*, ed. Günter Wein and Franziska Wein (Trier, 2011).

Michaelis, Herbert and Ernst Schraepler (eds), *Ursachen und Folgen. Vom deutschen Zusammenbruch 1918 und 1945 bis zur staatlichen Neuordnung Deutschlands in der Gegenwart. Eine Urkunden- und Dokumentensammlung zur Zeitgeschichte*, 27 vols (Berlin, 1958–79).

Moll, Martin (ed.), *'Führer-Erlasse' 1939–1945. Edition sämtlicher überlieferter, nicht im Reichsgesetzblatt abgedruckter, von Hitler während des Zweiten Weltkriegs schriftlich erteilter Direktiven aus den Bereichen Staat, Partei, Wirtschaft, Besatzungspolitik und Militärverwaltung* (Stuttgart, 1997).

Moltmann, Günter, 'Goebbels' Rede zum totalen Krieg am 18. Februar 1943', in *Vierteljahrshefte für Zeitgeschichte*, 12 (1964), 13–43.

Oldenhage, Klaus, 'Die Pfalz und das Saarland während des Krieges (1940–1945). Aus den Lageberichten des Oberlandesgerichtspräsidenten und Generalstaatsanwaltes in Zweibrücken', in *Jahrbuch für westdeutsche Landesgeschichte*, Part I: 5 (1979), 303–56, Part II: 6 (1980), 343–98.

Pötzl, Norbert F., *Casablanca 1943. Das geheime Treffen, der Film und die Wende des Krieges* (Munich, 2017).

Rebentisch, Dieter, *Führerstaat und Verwaltung im Zweiten Weltkrieg. Verfassungsentwicklung und Verfassungspolitik, 1939–1945* (Stuttgart, 1989).

Regenhardt, Hans Otto (ed.), *Forum Geschichte*, Parts 9/10: *Vom Kaiserreich bis zur Gegenwart* (Berlin, 2010).

Reuth, Ralf Georg, *Goebbels* (Munich/Zurich, 1990).

Ritter, Hans, *Der Zukunftskrieg und seine Waffen* (Leipzig, 1924).

Sauer, Michael (ed.), *Geschichte und Geschehen* (Stuttgart/Leipzig, 2013).

Schreier, Christa, 'Der Sportpalast in seiner baulichen Entwicklung', in Alfons Arenhövel (ed.), *Arena der Leidenschaften. Der Berliner Sportpalast und seine Veranstaltungen 1920–1973* (Berlin, 1990), 16–38.

Schütz, Hans (ed.), *Bamberger Berichte über Stimmung und Haltung der Bevölkerung des Oberlandesgerichtsbezirks Bamberg während des 2. Weltkrieges* (Bamberg, 1983).

Seligmann, Rafael, *Hitler. Die Deutschen und ihr Führer* (Berlin, 2004).
Soldan, George, *Der Mensch in der Schlacht der Zukunft* (Oldenburg, 1925).
Speer, Albert, *Erinnerungen* (Berlin, 1999).
Steinert, Marlis G., *Hitlers Krieg und die Deutschen. Stimmung und Haltung der deutschen Bevölkerung im Zweiten Weltkrieg* (Düsseldorf/Vienna, 1970).
Stumpf, Reinhard, 'Der Krieg im Mittelmeerraum 1942/43: Die Operationen in Nordafrika und im Mittelmeer', in Horst Boog et al. (eds), *Der Globale Krieg. Die Ausweitung zum Weltkrieg und der Wechsel der Initiative 1941–1943* (Stuttgart, 1990), 567–757.
Thacker, Toby, *Joseph Goebbels. Life and Death* (London, 2009).
Wegner, Bernd, 'Der Krieg gegen die Sowjetunion 1941/43', in Horst Boog et al. (eds), *Der Globale Krieg. Die Ausweitung zum Weltkrieg und der Wechsel der Initiative 1941–1943* (Stuttgart, 1990), 759–1102.

Index

For the benefit of digital users, indexed terms that span two pages (e.g., 52–53) may, on occasion, appear on only one of those pages.

6th Army 11, 14, 21, 25–26, 34–35, 45

Africa 8, 12–14, 16, 20–21, 36
Algeria 13, 16
Allies 13–14, 18, 20–21, 31–32,
    57–59, 101–102, 117
America/USA 31, 54
    forces 13, 16
    newspapers/press 88–90, 101–102
Andreas-Friedrich, Ruth 108
Anglo-Saxon
    armed forces 88
    powers 53
    states 54
annihilation 10, 17, 42–43, 51, 59–61,
    66–68
anti-Jewish/anti-Semitic
    attacks 57–59
    elements 111
    groups 57–59
    polemic 61
    policies 53, 57–59
    propaganda 116–117
    proposition 57
    tirades 59–61
armaments 23–24, 30, 42, 57, 72, 76,
    80–81, 83, 88–90, 94, 111, 119–121
atrocities 2, 18–21
Auschwitz 17, 111–112
Axis 16, 54, 58

Baarová, Lída 6–7
Baku 8, 16
Baltimore 101–102
Bamberg 105

Battle of Kunersdorf 87
Bavaria 104–105
Beaverbrook, Lord 50
Belgium 17
Berchtesgaden 113, 116
Berlin 4, 6, 10, 14, 28–30, 36, 39, 43,
    71–76, 83–84, 97–100, 108–116
Berlin Jews 39, 56–57, 111
Berlin Sports Palace 1–5, 12, 21, 24,
    30–34, 38–41, 44, 57–61, 88–90,
    97, 100–105, 108–109, 111, 115,
    117–118
Berne 99
Blitzkrieg 60
bolshevism/bolshevists 8, 21–22,
    32–33, 36, 42–43, 46–54, 56, 60,
    62, 64–67, 80–81, 84, 92, 100,
    108, 113
bolshevization 48, 50, 52, 54, 112
Bormann, Albert 26–27
Bormann, Martin 22–27, 29–30, 37,
    59–61, 113–114, 118–119, 121
Brandt, Karl 26–27
Brauchitsch, Walther von 10
Bremen 7–8
Breslau 118–119
Britain/England 8, 10, 19–21, 31, 50,
    52, 54, 56, 90–92, 98, 100, 112
    forces 13, 16
    Parliament 18
    press 56, 88–90, 101

Casablanca 8–9, 31–32
Caspian Sea 10
Christmas 21–22

Churchill, Winston 31
Cologne 7–8
Committee of Four 25, 30
Committee of Three 24–25, 28, 37, 113–115
communism/communists 12, 42–43, 52–54, 56, 62, 108, 115

Darré, Walther 115–116
deportation 17–18, 20–21, 39, 57, 109, 111–113
Dietl, Eduard 9–10, 27, 102
Dresden 109
Duisburg 7–8
Düsseldorf 7–8

East Asia 8, 88
eastern front 11, 14, 16, 19–21, 25, 36, 44, 56, 61–62, 76, 88–90, 92, 103, 107, 109, 117
Eastern Proclamation 67
East Indies 20
Egypt 7–8, 16, 19
  Cairo 8
El-Alamein 8, 12, 16
Essen 7–8
extermination 17–19, 57–59, 100–101

fascism 67, 88
Fetscher, Iring 109–110
film/cinema/theatre 4, 24, 31, 87, 95
Four-Year Plan 97–98
France/French 14, 17, 65
  forces 13
  North Africa 20
  occupiers 95
Franconia 105
Frederick the Great 86–87
Frick, Wilhelm 112–113, 115–116
Führer 3, 5–9, 14–15, 19, 22–24, 27–28, 30, 33–34, 36–37, 44–48, 50, 60, 67–70, 74, 76–78, 80, 86–88, 90–92, 94–98, 113–114, 118–120, see also Hitler
Funk, Walther 23, 25, 30, 113–114, 116

Gauleiters 4, 6, 10, 14, 18, 35–36, 38, 84, 97–98, 120, 122
Gayda, Virginio 101
George, Heinrich 42
German Labour Front (DAF) 22, 33, 42
German News Agency 100–101
Goebbels, Helga 98
Goebbels, Hilde 98
Goebbels, Joseph
  diaries 4–5, 7–9, 11–15, 18–19, 21–26, 30–32, 35–39, 42, 97, 99–100, 102, 106–116, 120–122
  'Our Will and Our Way' 35
  'The Earth's Blessing' 11
  'The European Crisis' 39
  'The Optics of the War' 24
  'The War as Social Revolution' 11
  'Total War' 24
Goebbels, Magda 83
Göring, Hermann 10, 29–30, 41, 59, 97–98, 113–114, 116, 119, 121
Gutterer, Leopold 19, 106–107

Hesse 108
Hierl, Konstantin 33
Himmler, Heinrich 6–7, 27, 33, 113, 119
Hitler, Adolf 5–10, 12–16, 18, 22–37, 41–42, 45, 59, 61, 65–67, 87, 100, 102–103, 111–122, see also Führer
Holstein 109
home front 2–3, 7, 14–15, 28, 39, 67, 81, 84, 88–92, 94, 99, 110, 117
Hotzel, Siegfried 109
Hungarians 36

India 19–20
international capitalist tyranny 49–51
Iran 8, 19–20
Iraq 8
Istanbul 100
Italians 36
Italy 31–32, 87–89, 99, 101

Japan 31–32, 87–89
Jewish
  communities 17, 112
  dwellings 112–113
  liquidation squads 52
  menace 58
  newspapers 56
  policy 17–21, 111–112
  press 88–90
  question 18, 20–21, 28–29, 39, 112
  slavery 50–51
  terrorism 46–48
  world conspiracy 53
Jews/Jewry 3, 17–21, 32–33, 36, 39,
    42–43, 49–52, 54, 56–61, 64, 90,
    100–101, 109, 111–113
Jordan 16

Keitel, Wilhelm 23–25, 113–115,
    118–119
Kenner, Friedrich 108
Klemperer, Victor 109
Klöpfer, Eugen 42
Kolberg 95
Körner, Hellmut 42, 97–98
Körner, Theodor 95
Krasny 16
Kremlin 48–50, 62
Kristallnacht 6–7

Lammers, Hans-Heinrich 23–25,
    29–30, 113–114, 118–121
Lanke 84
Laubach 108
Ley, Robert 22, 33, 42, 78, 94–95,
    97–98, 111, 113–114, 116
Libya 7–8
Liebel, Margarete 107
London 18, 50, 54, 98
Lübeck 7–8
Ludendorff, Erich 2–3

Majdanek 17
media 2, 4–5, 9, 12–13, 18, 20–22,
    31, 87, 98, 104–105, see also
    newspapers/press, newsreel, radio

Mediterranean 13–14
Mehs, Matthias Joseph 108–109
Memmingen 107
Mesopotamia 10
Milch, Erhard 42, 97–98
military
  action 86
  affairs 119
  campaigns 6–7
  catastrophe 21
  challenge 117
  danger 62
  defeats 7–8
  developments 32, 50
  difficulties 58
  information 21–22
  matters 119–120
  means 52–54
  news 16
  offices 74
  parades 13
  power 52, 56
  pressure 46–47
  protection 108
  reasons 8
  role 113–114
  service 76–78, 80–81
  setbacks 32–33
  significance 60
  situation 7–8, 25, 103
  strategy 31
  strength 54
  victory 9
Minetti, Bernhard 42
Montgomery, Bernard 16
Morocco 13, 16, 31
Moscow 20–21, 50
Munich 13, 111

Napoleon 95
National Socialism (NS) 12, 22, 40,
    44, 46, 107, 119
  activists 59–61, 90
  government 42–43, 70
  justice 66–68
  leadership 15, 64, 95

National Socialism (NS) (*cont.*)
  meetings 12–13
  movement 46–48, 56, 62, 68–70
  occupiers 51
  policy 12–13
  power structure 6–7
  propaganda 1, 87
  regime 67, 109–110
  state 46
  system 3
  version of 'total war' 17
National Socialist Party (NSDAP,
  Nazi Party) 1–2, 4, 13, 34,
  40–41, 43, 46–48, 57–59, 72–74,
  92, 95, 97, 100–101, 108, 115, 119
  Party Chancellery 18, 22, 59–61
National Socialists 6, 27, 32, 39–40,
  48–50, 52, 56, 78, 105–111
National Socialist Welfare 82
Near East 8, 16, 19–20
Netherlands 17, 109–110
Neureiter, Hertha 107
newspapers/press 1, 8–10, 18–21, 27,
  38–40, 45, 56, 84, 86, 88–90,
  98–102, 109
  Aftonbladet 100–101
  Baseler National-Zeitung 99
  Basler Nachrichten 99
  Berliner Tageblatt 52
  Boston Daily Globe 101–102
  Cumhuriyet 100
  Daily Express 101
  Daily Herald 101
  *Daily Telegraph and Morning
    Post* 101
  Das Reich 11–12, 22, 24, 30, 35, 39,
    65–67, 69, 108–109, 115, 118
  Der Bund 99
  Die Tat 99
  Die Welt 1
  Die Weltwoche 99
  Evening Sun 101–102
  Giornale d'Italia 101
  *Göteborgs Handels-och
    Sjöfatstidning* 100–101
  Manchester Guardian 101
  Neue Zürcher Zeitung 99–100

  New York Herald Tribune 101
  New York Times 101
  San Francisco Chronicle 101–102
  The Times 101
  Völkischer Beobachter 31, 40
  Vossische Zeitung 52
  Washington Post 101
  Yeni Sabah 100
  newsreel 1, 40, 42
  New York 101
Nordmann, Wilfried 109
Normandy 117
Norway 17
Nöthling, August 115–116
Nuremberg 46–48

Obersalzberg 117
Operation Reinhardt 17

Palestine 8, 16, 20
Paulus, Friedrich 34–35
Pausen, Agnes 109
plutocracy 11, 32–33, 56
plutocratic capitalism 53–54
plutocratic tyranny 88
Poland 17–20, 60, 65, 116–117
Pomerania 106
Posen (Poznań) 35–36, 120
propaganda 1–9, 11–13, 15–21,
  23–25, 31–32, 34–35, 40–41, 53,
  57–59, 65–67, 71–73, 76–78,
  87–91, 95, 98–105, 108, 110–112,
  115–117, 122
Propaganda Minister 1, 4, 6–7, 9, 18,
  20, 28–29, 46, 98, 101
Propaganda Ministry 29, 99
Propaganda Offices 12, 38, 102,
  106–107
Prussia 26, 86–87, 95, 121

radio 1, 8–10, 13, 18, 24, 31–33, 35,
  38, 40, 44, 59, 78, 90, 103–105,
  107
rallies 1–5, 12–13, 33–34, 38–42, 44,
  46–48, 90, 95, 97–98, 102–103,
  108–110
Rastenburg 36

Red Army 9, 11, 28, 117
Reich Chancellery 23, 37, 118–120
Reichsleiters 10, 35–36, 97
Ribbentrop, Joachim von 6–7, 115–116
Richthofen, Wolfram von 102
Röhm, Ernst 6
Romanians 36
Rome 117
Rommel, Erwin 8, 12–14, 16
Roosevelt, Franklin D. 31–32
Rosenberg, Alfred 67
Rostock 7–8
Russia 7, 60–61, 100, see also Soviet Union

Sauckel, Fritz 23, 25, 30, 35–36, 42, 94–95
Saxony 106–107
Schmundt, Rudolf 26–27
Schwanenwerder 83
Security Service (SD) 12–13, 15, 33
Seligmann, Rafael 1
Seven Years' War 87
Siberian tundra 50
Slovakian Jews 17
Soviet Union 6–7, 9–11, 14, 17, 34–35, 47–50, 52–54, 60, 65, 67, 108, 116–117, see also Russia
Speer, Albert 23, 29–30, 42–43, 94–95, 97–98, 113–114, 116–119
SS 12, 27, 33, 39, 111
Stalingrad 8–12, 14–16, 21, 25–31, 34–36, 44–45, 60–61, 86–89, 117
Stalin, Joseph 48–50, 108

Steppe 46–48, 50, 60, 88
Stuckart, Wilhelm 42, 97–98
Sudeten crisis 6–7, 41
summer offensive 4–39, 67–70, 86, 88, 117
Swabia 105–106
Sweden 18–19, 100–101
Switzerland 102
newspapers 99–100
Syria 16

Thierack, Otto Georg 42, 97–98
Third Silesian War 86
Tobruk 7–8
Tunisia 13–14

Vienna 28–29
Vinnitsa 8, 11, 14, 44

Wars of Liberation 95
Washington 18, 31, 50, 101
Wehrmacht 23–24, 26–27, 46–49, 88–90, 94, 114, 117–118, 120–122
Wehrmacht High Command (OKW) 21, 23, 25, 109–110
Weimar Republic 6, 40–41
Westphalia 106
Winter Aid 10, 41
winter crisis 4, 7, 16, 25–26, 117
Wittlich 108–109
Wolff, Karl 27

Zeitzler, Kurt 27–28
Zweibrücken 105–106